The Art of Freedom

Kiss Your Job Goodbye, Build an Online Tribe, Leave a Legacy

by Jesse Panama

Dad,

We lost you before publication,

but your DNA is all over this book and everything I do.

Table of Contents

You're not free.
It's time we changed that.
This is how we're going to do it.

Introduction

Hidden in plain sight is a soul-sucking, global epidemic that very likely finds you:

- Working five days a week so that you can enjoy the other two
- Working 50 weeks a year so that you can have two weeks of vacation
- Building someone else's dream instead of your own
- Not having a baseline of freedom that allows you to live the life and make the impact that your heart desires

This epidemic is known as the 9 to 5.

And what makes it even more dangerous?

Everyone else thinks it's NORMAL.

Not only would society (and likely your family) have you believe that this is a perfectly acceptable way for you to live; they encourage it.

But you know what? It's not their fault. And it's certainly not yours, either. The real question to ask yourself is, why did you choose this path? Or more to the point, did you choose this path, or did this path choose you?

The "Magic Pot" Parable

A young woman is preparing a pot roast while her friend looks on. She cuts off both ends of the roast, prepares it and puts it in the pan. "Why do you cut off the ends?" her friend asks. "I don't know," she replies. "My mother always did it that way and I learned how to cook it from her."

Her friend's question made her curious about her pot roast preparation. During her next visit home, she asked her mother, "How do you cook a pot roast?" Her mother proceeded to explain and added, "You cut off both ends, prepare it and put it in the pot and then in the oven." "Why do you cut off the ends?" The daughter asked. Baffled, the mother offered, "That's how my mother did it and I learned it from her!"

Her daughter's inquiry made the mother think more about the pot roast preparation. When she next visited her mother in the nursing home, she asked, "Mom, how do you cook a pot roast?" Her mother slowly answered, thinking between sentences. "Well, you prepare it with spices, cut off both ends and put it in the pot." The mother asked, "But why do you cut off the ends?" The grandmother's eyes sparkled as she remembered. "Well, the roasts were always bigger than the pot that we had back then. I had to cut off the ends to fit it into the pot that I owned."

While you may not be cutting off pot roast ends anytime soon, ask yourself: what have you unknowingly cut off in your own life? Could it be your happiness? Your peace of mind? Your **freedom**? Cuts pretty deep, right?!

"Entrepreneurial Revolution?" Really?!

Conventional "wisdom" would have you believe that more people than ever are starting new businesses, and that a greater percentage of these businesses than ever achieve success.

The facts, however, paint a very different picture:

- According to the 2017 Kaufman Activity Index, the number of new business startups actually **decreased** during the 20-year period from 1996 to 2016, and at **no time** surpassed the 1996 level even briefly.

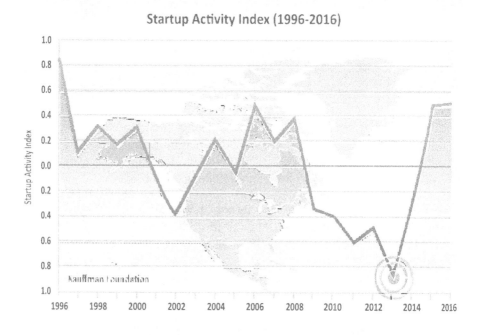

- According to the U.S. Bureau of Labor Statistics, the 20% success rate of new businesses (defined as lasting more than one year) has remained virtually unchanged since **1995**.

But Here's the Good News

There's another "epidemic" taking place right now that's far more positive and inspiring and is only going to grow more powerful in the years to come. Quietly taking shape is a new wave of soulful, heart-centered, cerebral entrepreneurs who blend several key elements into a new kind of freedom lifestyle called the *Ultimate Vida* (more on that in a moment!).

According to a Fortune Magazine article detailing a CB Insights survey, the number one reason why businesses fail is due to lack of market need. In real talk, this simply means that people have to want what you're offering them.

The Ultimate Vida way of entrepreneurship lets you make sure they will — ethically, with love and kindness, giving you an unfair advantage that'll make you feel like you're wearing 3D glasses. Your people will feel like you've got their backs, and you know them better than they know themselves.

You Are Ready for This

Whether you know it or not, you're in an awesome – almost perfect – place to kiss the 9 to 5 goodbye and pursue your freedom lifestyle! Everything you've accomplished so far (yes, accomplished — you should be proud of yourself!) has led you to this point and has been secretly preparing you behind the scenes.

While the rare high school drop-outs who become mega-successful get glorified, you know what's a far more common scenario with a much higher success rate? Doing *what you've already done* – developing the professional and emotional foundation that prepares you to strategically take the leap.

You've cultivated tangible, industry-specific skills that you can very likely apply to your entrepreneurial ventures, even if you don't yet see how. And just as importantly, you've honed vital intangible skills such as communication, teamwork and negotiation, which are going to serve you extremely well.

And even more valuable? You've discovered exactly what you *don't* want – which is a life of normalcy and limits, while building someone else's dream (your boss's or your company's) instead of your own.

The Even Better News: Entrepreneurs Are Happier

Many people have the (false) perception that the unpredictability of being an entrepreneur leads to greater stress and anxiety. The data, however, says otherwise. It turns out that entrepreneurs are happier and healthier (both physically and mentally) than their employee counterparts.

- A Baylor University and Louisiana State University joint study combining data from the Center for Disease Control and the US Census found that as the number of small businesses in a given area increased, **the health of the surrounding community improved**.

- A personal research project conducted by author James Clear concluded that entrepreneurs have a **significantly lower incidence of physical and mental illnesses**, visit the hospital less often, and report higher levels of life satisfaction.

- A survey of 11,000 graduates of The Wharton School of The University of Pennsylvania revealed entrepreneurship to be the **biggest predictor of happiness**.

- A Forbes Magazine article featured a global research study led by Babson College, in which researchers spoke to a whopping 197,000 people in 70 different countries. The data showed that whether they run early-stage startups or established businesses, entrepreneurs in all regions **rated their own well-being higher** than their employee counterparts.

Time for Some Real Talk

I'm not saying it's better or more noble to be an entrepreneur. In fact, I have enormous respect for those who put in a hard day's work as employees and provide for their families. Without employees, entrepreneurs couldn't exist. And vice versa. It's an integral, symbiotic relationship.

But let's keep it real, shall we? Would you have really picked up this book if you were content living the 9 to 5? Don't you crave the ability to set your own schedule, work from anywhere, and take back the reins of your life? Don't you burn inside to be the captain of your own ship and the architect of your own destiny? Don't you yearn to play a bigger game, make a greater impact, and leave a loftier legacy? While your head says "I'm good where I'm at, doesn't your heart scream "There is so much more, and my time is NOW?!"

This Book is Your Roadmap

I realize it's a bold, audacious statement to declare this book your roadmap. But it's a statement I'm prepared to back up and earn your trust with, in the chapters and pages that follow.

On May 15, 1998, I left the only adult job I've ever had, and began my entrepreneurial journey. So, this year, on May 15, 2020, I celebrated my 22-year Freedom Anniversary! I don't say this to brag. On the contrary, I'm no smarter or more special than you are. There are only two reasons that my story should matter to you.

One, I've done this for 22 years. More than two decades that have spanned a variety of economies, trends, and technological eras. I've done it with several different businesses and business models, with teams and alone, from home and while traveling. I started it well before social media was a thing, and built and sustained it with no roadmap whatsoever. (I would have killed for this book when I started!)

So, I'll be teaching you timeless strategies and tactics that are not based on some trend or fad, but that will be as relevant five or 10 or 20 years from now as they are today (plus, I'll give you links that will be constantly updated). Oh, and Internet years are kind of like dog years, so my 22 years doing this is really more like 154 – just sayin. ☺

Two, I'm not going anywhere, and I'll be there for you every step of the way. I am making it my mission and life's work to empower and guide you and other epic people around the world just like you to discover, create and sustain your freedom lifestyle. Your *Ultimate Vida*.

But we're going to go several steps beyond entrepreneurship. Most people believe that once they make the leap and become their own boss, it's the be all and end all. Spoiler alert: it's not. You'll ride the wave for a while, but then there will be an existential crash of sorts, where you ask yourself "OK, now what?"

But you're not going to have that crash. You're going to deftly sidestep it with the help of this book, and ongoing support and resources you'll have access to. We're going to anticipate your journey together, and have you playing chess while others play checkers – always a move or two ahead. How are we going to do that? Well, because our real mission here is to design...

Your Masterpiece Life

Remember a moment ago, when I mentioned that there's a new wave of heart-centered, cerebral entrepreneurs taking shape? That's where the real magic starts, and that's the real game we're playing here – crafting your ideal path that is uniquely yours to get you there. Of course, you'll build a business and/or tap into other freedom-based models for making money. But we're going to take it deeper than that. Aside from business, I'm also going to point you in the direction of vital, life-changing things you can learn about elements like travel, mindset, language, health & wellness and more.

Warning: By going through this process, it's highly likely you'll become a Renaissance Man or Woman of sorts. You may suddenly be seen as an International Man/Woman of Mystery; James Bond-esque, or Lara Croft-esque, if you will. You will almost certainly be seen as more charismatic and magnetic to whomever you'd like to attract. Basically, you'll exude a whole new cool factor and *je ne sais quoi*. That's not why we're doing this, but it's likely to happen, so I want you to be prepared. ☺

So why, then, are we doing this? Two words: *blank canvas*. We want to create a clean slate for you where all things are possible, and you can mold your life into anything you want it to be. I believe this kind of life is only possible if freedom becomes your new baseline. And I'm pretty sure you believe that, too.

It's Deeply Personal

My original motives for creating my own freedom lifestyle? I loved to travel and couldn't stand the idea of having a boss. Rather simple, and more than enough to fuel my fire.

But once I started to grow and evolve as a person, I realized I wanted — no, *needed* — to light the path for others. That's when the idea to create Ultimate Vida was born!

But the past few years? They've brought me to my knees, and that's putting it mildly. For now, I'll reveal that my dad's been battling some major health challenges. And only because my Ultimate Vida was in place have I been able to spend weeks and months at a time with my parents, rather than the few days here and there I would've been restricted to with a normal job and lifestyle. Not only has this resulted in providing far more hands-on help than would typically be possible, but our relationship has deepened tremendously. Money alone does NOT equal freedom. A challenging time has been profoundly beautiful — all because Ultimate Vida is the baseline.

So, our mission is to create the space for you to create the impact and legacy that you want your life to stand for. We want to design your Masterpiece Life; your Magnum Opus. Your **Ultimate Vida**. *That* is why we're doing this.

This is going to be the ride of your life! I'm so excited for you, and I stand in awe and gratitude that I get to be a small part of your story. Turn the page, and let's get going! ☺

To **your** Ultimate Vida,

-Jesse

Your Blueprint for a Successful Jailbreak

Here's how I'm going to put the blueprint together for you.

For each step, I'm going to give you a set of targets — action steps that you have to complete.

If you complete them, and then keep building on that success, then you WILL break free, and your life will never be the same again.

But you MUST complete the action steps.

If you don't complete the action steps, you're not actually trying to escape - you're just entertaining yourself by imagining a different life. Which is fine, if that's what you want — but why not go a little further and actually make it happen?

Step 1: Can you even break out of this joint?

You're in a prison that I broke out of over 20 years ago, back when technology was limited and there was no roadmap. Today, technology is more robust than ever, but amazingly, there's still no roadmap. That's why I wrote this book. I'm going to tell you exactly how I got out, and show you how to make your escape today and change your life forever.

Step 2: You're not going to get out on your own

Most people who want to break free are lonely — the other prisoners tell them that jail life is normal, and they don't spend time with anyone on the outside. I'm going to show you how other people will become your greatest strength and help you achieve everything you dream of — but in a way you might not be expecting.

Step 3: How to find the inner strength to escape

Being different is difficult. Breaking norms is difficult. Escaping — really escaping — is no walk in the park. But there's a Japanese concept that will give you the steel core that will make your victory inevitable.

Step 4: Putting the team together

In Step 2, I show you how other people are your greatest strength. In Step 4, I show you how you can multiply that by a factor of 10x or 100x, and how the remarkable power of people in networks can change your life forever.

Step 5: Which way should this tunnel go?

You've understood the importance of other people, and you learned how to put a team together. Now it's time to work out which way the tunnel is going. In other words, what exactly are you going to focus on? You're not going to try and be all things to all people — you're going to become a specialist — but you're going to do it in a very particular way.

Step 6: Can you make that guard a friend?

If you can find out everything possible about one of the prison guards, you might be able to turn them into a friend — and that can make or break a prison escape. In this step, I'm going to show you how to understand people in more detail than you've ever done before, and how that will make them eager to help you escape.

Step 7: Knowing everybody's routine

You've got a team, you've planned where the tunnel is going, you've got a friend among the guards — now it's time to make sure you know everyone's routine down to the tiniest possible detail. This is where you use tools that I show you to know more about the people in the team you've built than they even know about themselves — and that's part of why they'll grow to trust and confide in you.

Step 8: Ready, steady, GO — but don't get caught!

You're ready to make a bid for freedom now — and this step shows you how to use the unusual power of storytelling and dominoes to make sure that nobody can rip you off. It will make you impossible to copy — and impossible for the cops to know where you're hidden... ☺

Step 9: Staying in touch on the outside

You're out — but that's just the beginning. There's so much more you can achieve, once you master how to communicate with the team you've built. This is where they begin to turn into a tribe, and where you learn how to create new levels of value (and achieve new levels of success).

Step 10: You've done it — now how do you stay free?

You've earned the right to focus on the big picture now — and as you become more skilled at building strategies, your tactics will become even more effective. This is the step where I start to show you how to think on a higher level, that will let you expand the boundaries of your world as far as you want to.

Step 11: Putting cash in the bank (not robbing it)

If you've implemented all the tasks I've given you by this point in the book, you've built what will become your new life. But (and this is why you've built it more successfully than other people) you haven't made any money out of it yet. This is where that changes.

Step 12: The map that will take you to safety

You've done the big stuff. Now we get into the magic that comes with detailed instructions. By this point, you're ready for the crunchy stuff, and I'm going to start by showing you the incredible importance of first impressions — how (and where!) to make them.

Step 13: Buying off the cops — you'll never get arrested again

Some people think they can stay ahead of the game by hustling — by working all the time on blog posts and social media and guest posting and Instagram and the next big thing and so on forever. I'm going to show you how to cut through all that insanity in the simplest way possible — by setting up a machine where for every dollar you put in, you get more than a dollar back — sometimes *much* more.

Step 1: Can You Even Break Out of This Joint?

This is my story — to show you it's possible, and give you the key checkpoints for **your own** jailbreak.

My Story, Your Purpose

This is where I get to do something I never thought I'd do: tell you my story.

Originally, I'd planned on launching straight into the strategies and techniques for crafting your Ultimate Vida, but I realized that would've been a major mistake for a few reasons.

First, it's only natural that you're more likely to take to heart and implement the strategies and tactics I share with you if we form a genuine bond.

Plus, these bonds and connections are at the very core of who I am and what Ultimate Vida is. I have so much love for you and I am rooting for you so hard, you have no idea. And I'm not just talking from afar or on a collective basis. I'm talking YOU. I genuinely hope that you and I get the opportunity to trade stories one day over a cup of coffee or glass of wine.

Second, I strongly believe that we are all mirrors of each other. My story is no more special or significant than yours, but I do believe you'll be able to see parts of yourself in my story and relate them to your own (I'll help you do this), which is really what it's all about.

Uncovering Your Tapestry of Why

Third, it's trendy these days for leaders and teachers to talk about finding your "why" and making it your driving force behind everything you do. But I don't feel it's nearly that black and white. I believe your "why" is more of a tapestry of factors, stories and moments in your life. And I believe my story (and by extension, yours) will help you weave your own unique Ultimate Vida tapestry that will become your North Star – your ultimate why.

As I tell my story, I'll have several highlighted areas where I ask you questions to relate my story to your own life, and events that shaped you.

It is crucial that each time you read one of these highlighted sections, you pause, consider these moments, events, or feelings that occurred in your life, and fully allow yourself to "go there" mentally and emotionally.

Once you've "gone there," note down absolutely everything you can remember about these moments or experiences – most importantly, your thoughts and feelings about them, and any inner conflict you may have felt. Write in free form with no pausing, editing, or judgment. There will be plenty of time to go back and review your answers later. But for now, simply know that they will form your "Tapestry of Why" and play a central and crucial role in your story, and where it goes from here!

With that said, let's do this!

The Ultimate Vida Began in the Womb

Ultimate Vida, and this book, in a very real sense, all started in the womb.

Much to my mom's chagrin, I asserted my independence and began my trend of bucking conventional norms before I was even born – a fact that she frequently reminds me of! I was born exactly 14 no doubt excruciating days for my mom after my due date. Little did any of us know that it was a serious harbinger of what would come in the years that followed. And by "years that followed," I mean my *entire life*.

> *Looking back, were there any very early events that shaped your life's direction or desires before you were consciously able to participate? They don't have to be from the womb (I tend to go to extremes!), but go back as far as you can remember.*
>
> *If you can't answer this question from memory, ask your family! They are a great resource. Note these down here, as they might be far more relevant than you think! Often, those early, "instinctive" inclinations represent our truest self.*

California Dreamin'

Womb aside, the earliest tangible sign of Ultimate Vida taking shape was when I became enchanted with California at the ripe old age of four and promptly announced to my parents that one day I would move there and live on the ocean. I don't know if it was something I saw on TV or in the movies, but I was spellbound. There was just something about the beach, the lifestyle, and the west coast that captivated me, even before I was capable of understanding, well – anything.

No, it wasn't a foreign land, and didn't have the international flair that Ultimate Vida would come to stand for. But looking back, it was definitely a herald of things to come. Plus, give me a break – I was four freaking years old. And unlike Star Wars and cops & robbers, my California obsession proved to have staying power (although I still kinda dig Star Wars!).

Sports was another constant of my childhood, and for some inexplicable reason, I became a die-hard Los Angeles Lakers fan, even as I grew up in the northern Virginia suburbs of Washington, DC. I was entranced by the Lakers' "showtime" brand of basketball in the 1980s orchestrated by Magic Johnson (and I may or may not have also been taken by the stars and celebrities that attended the games).

At several points during my childhood, I excitedly announced to my parents (and anyone else who would listen) that one day I would move out west and live in California. They always smiled and were supportive, but I'm sure they were thinking it was a phase that would pass. And who could blame them? Most kids my age wanted to be pirates or astronauts, so by that measure, moving to California is fairly innocuous, right?

*What's the earliest memory you have of knowing you wanted
to play a bigger game? To live a different kind of life? To make
your own rules? I'm not talking infancy here; I'm talking your
earliest personal memories, when you became a real human
being and began to form independent thoughts* ☺

Extending the borders... Ultimate Vida Goes Global

It's 1985. I'm 10 years old. And my parents announce to my brother and me that we will be traveling to Indonesia that summer.

Say whaaaat? I'm not even sure I had heard of Indonesia at that point. Sure, I was an adventurer and explorer at heart, even at that young age. But suffice it to say, for a kid growing up in the suburbs of Washington, D.C. who took a solid few years before eating anything other than peanut butter and crackers, Indonesia was quite literally way out there. And while I was excited, I also remember feeling somewhat scared and nervous.

Quick back story: if you think I'm an adventurer, my uncle Lincoln puts me (and just about everyone else) to shame. I mean, the dude started his Ultimate Vida in the nineteen freaking sixties! He met a wonderful Taiwanese woman whom he fell in love with (and who became my aunt), and they lived in various parts of Asia and Europe while he was a traveling journalist. Oh, and all this while raising three amazing kids who are my dear cousins. How cool is that?

Anyway, in 1985, they were living in Jakarta, Indonesia, and for whatever reason, my parents decided it was time we pay them a visit. And if the seed was planted with my California dreaming that started at age four? Looking back, I'd say in Indonesia, it was starting to blossom at age 10 without me even realizing it yet.

Now don't get me wrong; I was not some international sophisticate at age 10 in Indonesia. Far from it. There was still the little boy in me who craved his comforts. I remember there was a "Club America" in Jakarta (Indonesia's capital city), which my brother and I would lobby our parents to go to. There, we could enjoy "our" food, music and movies. So worldly, right?!

But there was another side of young Jesse beginning to take shape as well. I was fascinated with the street life and exotic nature of Indonesia. In fact, I was so inspired that I crafted a long letter to my best friend at the time, Matt. My letter was replete with dramatic tales of this faraway land, and soaring visions of the world travelers and explorers that we would become. I wish I still had that letter. Maybe Matt does, somewhere. It was classic, and it most definitely portended what was to come.

In that letter, young Jesse was honing his Ultimate Vida chops! The letter read like a fantasy tale, as if we were action heroes in a movie. But there was still something missing. Still another level to reach. How could I turn my dreams and desires in that letter into a deeper reality that I could actually do something about? Well...

What was your first trip to a "faraway land?" It need not be international. Just take yourself back to the first time you visited a place that felt foreign. It could be a different state, a different city, or a camping trip. Anywhere that the way of life was different than what you were used to.

What did you observe? How did it make you feel? Did anything inspire you? Leave a strong impression on you? Did you start to see and feel expanded possibilities for what your life could become?

Balinese Mountain Climbing: My First Epiphany

The other memory from that trip that really stuck with me is when we all took a side trip to Bali. And we're talking Bali in the 1980s, decades before it would become a hipster destination thanks to "Eat, Pray, Love" and the "new age" movement.

My coolest "normal memory" of that side trip is that the plane we flew over on was practically empty, save for a few affable Australians. So my brother, cousins and I got to run gleefully up and down the aisles in mid-flight. Air travel was a *lot* more relaxed back then.

On the deeper side? The more majestic side? The *Ultimate Vida* side?

I'll never forget the hike that my dad, my brother and I took. This hike is firmly entrenched in major family lore territory. The way I remember it, we hiked to the top of a large mountain. More likely, it was a small to medium sized hill, but why sweat the details, right? ☺

What is indisputable, though, is that on this hike, I connected with my "deeper self" for the first time in my life. It was the first time I was in true awe and wonder, not from the latest movie, sporting event, or action hero, but from an energetic force.

I was nowhere near evolved or developed enough to understand what was going on, but I do distinctly remember feeling a powerful energetic force on that "mountain." Like something so much bigger than myself was going on. That's where I had my first "spiritual experience," if you will. Where I felt for the first time on a visceral level that I could do and be anything I wanted in this lifetime.

And if you look closely enough in the photo below? You can see this awe, wonder and knowingness in my face (I'm Big Bro on the right). This is one of my very favorite pictures from my childhood, and is one of those times where a picture really is worth an *infinite* amount of words.

> *What is your first memory of connecting with your deeper self? Note: This book is NOT about religion or spirituality. I respect your belief system, whatever it is (as long as you do right by others).*
>
> *I simply want to take you back to your first moment of complete awe and wonder that you can remember. Your first memory of connecting with some deeper force beyond what your logical and rational mind could process. What was your first epiphany?*

From Jakarta to London: The James Bond Lifestyle?

Apparently, the Indonesia trip convinced my parents that they could travel to faraway lands with my brother and me in tow (until then, we had mostly just taken driving and camping trips). So, two summers later, we took a family vacation to England! And while it wasn't nearly as exotic as Indonesia, it had its own profound impact on me and Ultimate Vida.

I distinctly remember on the flight over seeing people in suits and business attire, and asking my parents why they were dressed like that, and being told, "Well, they are probably business travelers."

I asked, "You mean they have their own business, or they work for someone else?" They said, "It could be either," and my mind started spinning. I felt a surge of excitement, wondering what it would be like to live the dynamic lifestyle of an international businessman.

As you can imagine, seeing London for the first time made quite an impression on me. To this day, I'd say that London has an "electric" sort of buzz that's matched by very few cities in the world; cities like New York, Hong Kong and Tokyo. I was struck as a youngster how on one hand, it didn't seem so different than other big cities I'd seen; yet on the other, there was an unmistakably international flair. I was particularly taken with the British accent, which I had only heard on TV and in the movies before that trip.

And speaking of the movies? One of my most vivid memories from that trip involved a certain cinematic icon by the name of Bond... *James Bond* (said in my best Sean Connery voice).

As luck would have it, our trip coincided with opening night of the latest James Bond film, *The Living Daylights*. And let me tell you, going to the movies in London was on a whole other level than any theatre I'd been to in the states. First of all, there was actually an age limit, and it wasn't even an R-rated movie. Somehow, I was barely old enough to go, and my brother narrowly missed the cutoff, even though we were only three years apart. So, my mom and brother planned their own night on the town, and my dad took me to *The Living Daylights* premiere.

Man, when we walked into the theatre, I was in awe. It blew away any theatre I'd ever seen. It felt more like we were going to a concert or sporting event than a movie. There was a buzz and electricity in the air in anticipation of Bond's latest escapades being unveiled.

Needless to say, I was riveted by the movie. And surprise, surprise — I kind of had a new hero. I know my James Bond obsession sounds somewhat shallow compared to my Bali mountaintop epiphanies. But come on, I was a 12-year old kid at opening night in London, and here was this larger than life character who drove the coolest cars, wooed the most beautiful women, and had a sophistication and *je ne sais quoi* that was unmatched. Can you really blame me?!

That's when this notion of the "James Bond Lifestyle" started swimming around in my active but still largely undeveloped mind. Not so much being a special agent, but traveling in style, being an international man of mystery, and having that unmistakable "it factor."

In fact, looking back, I think that's the first time I really pondered the concept of charisma. It would prove to be the first time of many. Aside from his daring exploits, Bond had a certain magnetism that drew people to him, and I remember wondering to myself how I could develop a personality that drew people to me as well. *I would later discover that it's not so much about the personality as it is the life you lead and the impact you make...*

When was the first time you pondered the concept of charisma? Magnetism? Influence? Of causing people to feel a certain way based on your words, actions, or personality? When did you start thinking about the implications this could have on your lifestyle and life choices? This question is a bit more abstract and open ended, but it's a crucial one, so don't skip over it! ☺

Teenage Escapades: The Awkward Gets Awkwarder

(Oops, I just invented a word.)

I'd always known on some level that I wanted to be an entrepreneur. My childhood fascination with "business travelers" may have started it all. But it went way deeper than that. My trips to Indonesia and England took it to the next level, as I described. Looking back, I don't think I was cognizant or developed enough as a 10 or 12-year-old kid to consciously know I wanted to be an "entrepreneur." But I definitely did know I wanted to be FREE. Looking back, it didn't take a rocket scientist to see where things were going…

After those trips, my teenage years were suddenly upon me, whether I was ready or not. In some ways, I was a fairly normal teenage boy, with girls, sports and cars chief among my interests. Posters of Michael Jordan, Cindy Crawford, and a red Ferrari (but not just any red Ferrari – it was the one from my favorite TV show, Magnum P.I.!) adorned my walls.

But behind the scenes, there was another script running. I was fast becoming obsessed with business and direct marketing. Or to put it more crudely (and accurately), I was fast becoming obsessed with "biz ops" and "get rich quick schemes." I would pore through classified ads in the back of magazines promising wealth and riches, and call the 800 number to hear the recorded message or send in a "S.A.S.E." (Self Addressed Stamped Envelope) to the address listed for more information. Remember, websites were not yet a thing!

Before I knew it, I was on all kinds of mailing lists for business opportunities and get rich quick schemes. Little did the purveyors of said schemes know that they were dealing with a kid who wasn't even old enough to drive. To my parents' credit, they passed along these rapidly growing stacks of mail to me without much discussion. They probably figured it was a passing fad I was going through.

Turns out, this obsession was here to stay. But thankfully, it was beginning to change form. Initially, I was seduced by the actual content of these ads – the promise of overnight riches. I tried all sorts of crazy things. Chain letters, selling books through the mail, 900 numbers, you name it. Fortunately, I discovered fairly quickly how ludicrous these "opportunities" were. In fact, in one of my more lucid teenage moments, I distinctly remember at one point feeling angry that these companies were in business. I remember thinking that it's one thing for a teenager like me to temporarily fall for these false promises, but what about grown men and women who have families to feed and who are "investing" money they don't really have in search of that lifeline?

Anyway, once I realized that the opportunities themselves were generally bogus, I found myself nonetheless still fascinated by the marketing process behind them. I remember thinking to my young self how powerful it was that tiny classified ads or letters in the mail could get me to spend so much of my time – and more to the point, my allowance money – to uncover their secrets!

> *When did you first start thinking about business or marketing or making money? Did thoughts of having your own business ever cross your mind as a child or teenager, or was it strictly in the context of getting a job and earning a big paycheck?*

The Money-Making Lightbulb Switches On (Major Ah-ha Moment!)

So, my interest shifted — from the opportunities themselves to the words behind them. I began studying how these hooks, headlines and stories were crafted from a marketing and persuasion standpoint. That's making me sound way more advanced than I actually was. But it's nonetheless what I was doing in some form. And that's when I had my next "Ah-ha" moment. I remember it like it was yesterday...

I was holed up in my room one day after school, studying my latest collection of mail. By this point, it was pretty much a daily thing, as once you got on those "bizop" lists, it was "Katy, bar the door!" (channeling my dad there – that's one of his favorite expressions!).

Anyway, on this particular day, with Def Leppard's "Hysteria" playing in the background, young Jesse was reverse engineering his latest marketing funnel. *It was at least a decade before I understood what reverse engineering or a marketing funnel was, but I digress.* ☺

I remember distinctly the headline of the offer du jour being "How to make $4,000 per day sitting at your kitchen table in your underwear" (authored by Jeff Paul, whom I would see speak at a Dan Kennedy seminar a decade later). And as I read through Jeff's brilliantly crafted sales letter, that's when the light bulb went off.

I'd always loved writing and aspirational storytelling. Hence my soaring prose in my letter to Matt from Indonesia. And I'd now developed an (unhealthy?) obsession with direct marketing. I wasn't really comfortable with that obsession, though, because I knew on some level that most of the opportunities being peddled were sleazy and that these very skilled marketers were preying on people's hopes and dreams. And yet I couldn't look away. It was like a bad car wreck that demanded my attention. I powerlessly went further down the rabbit hole, until...BOOM! **Another epiphany**:

What if I figured out a way to combine my love of writing and my fascination with marketing to use these skills for good? What if I figured out a way to use them to create a freedom lifestyle for myself, while marketing legitimate solutions that would actually help people and improve their lives? In that moment, witnessed by Michael Jordan and Cindy Crawford, set to a Def Leppard soundtrack, the seed was officially planted.

What was your first specific "Ah-ha moment" that was not just an abstract energy or feeling, but a tangible vision where you could see the skeleton of a business or money making plan take shape? Note: Maybe you haven't had one yet, and if so, that's perfectly OK.

Maybe you grew up envisioning a more conventional life. Maybe this book is your aha moment, and if so, I'm honored. It's just as valuable (if not more!) to discover what we don't want as what we do want.

From High School to College: Four Amazing Years Deeper Down the Rabbit Hole

I didn't just like or enjoy my four years of college. I **freaking loved** them. They were four of the best years of my life and I'll always treasure them. I went to Syracuse University in upstate New York, and I can't recommend it enough. It was the perfect blend of academics, social life, sports, and just learning how to live and figure shit out. To this day, whenever I talk about my college years, it's with awe and reverence.

College is the one time in life where we have all the freedom of being an adult, without the responsibility. F.R.E.E.D.O.M. By the way, shouldn't those seven letters be sounded out into a song, just like Aretha Franklin's R.E.S.P.E.C.T.? Just sayin.

I was like a kid in a candy store with my newfound freedom. For the first time in my life, I was firmly in control of my own time and had no one weighing in on a constant basis about what I should be doing.

I had a strong "freedom realization" pretty early on in the college game. I realized that I wanted to do whatever possible to make this freedom not just a four-year blip on the radar in the grand scheme of my life, but use it to set the stage for freedom becoming a way of life.

This took a few different forms:

First, my obsession with direct marketing endured, as I continued sending away for all kinds of biz ops and marketing schemes in the mail. But I now took it to a new level. I started sending away for finance and health-related offers and offers in other industries as well. Because the point was not to buy the product being offered (though I may or may not have done that a few times;), but to understand the marketing behind these offers, and why they work.

Second, when it came time to declare my major, I chose to be a double major in marketing and finance. I remember feeling like this was a very cool moment – officially declaring to the world that I was going to be a businessman! Not surprisingly, my version of being a businessman was somewhat different than most of my friends and fellow business-major students, who dreamed of landing a job with one of the big accounting or consulting firms after we graduated.

Third, and most exciting, I took one of the first courses in entrepreneurship ever offered at any university! This was easily my favorite business-related course I took at college (my other favorite courses were writing, psychology and sociology, in case you're wondering). I still remember Professor Wilemon, extolling to us the virtues and challenges of being in business for ourselves, with his charming southern accent. I was riveted. It was all coming together.

Surprisingly, my most powerful declaration and foreshadowing of what was to come did not take place in any business-related course, but rather in a writing course that I took. One of the exercises was to write an essay on what our life was going to look like in five years. I remember tackling this essay with gusto – writing in vivid detail how in five short years, I would live by the beach in California and own my own business, at the ripe old age of 24 (I was 19 at the time). I remember showing the essay to my roommate and good friend Ajay, and it made quite an impression on him. Ajay remains a good friend, and to this day, whenever we hang out, he brings up that essay and graciously says "Look at you man, you actually followed through and did it."

> *When the first time you lived on your own, either at college or otherwise? Did you notice any change in your thinking or your visions for your life? Did you ever think what your life could be like if you made your own hours and set your own rules, rather than following someone else's? Did you ever imagine how magical your life could be if freedom became your new baseline?*

To MBA or not MBA: My Inner (and Outer) Conflict Continues

As I continued through my college years, I only became more resolute that going into business for myself was really what called to me. I knew in my mind and my heart that being an entrepreneur was the life I wanted. Yet inside, I still somehow felt conflicted. I knew that my parents had worked very hard to send me to college. They started putting money away in a college fund from the day I was born, and steadily contributed to it little by little during my childhood and high school years. And I knew they certainly didn't send me to college just so I could go into business for myself, which did NOT require the degree I was earning.

On some level, I think I also had some insecurity, if I'm being honest. What if I was romanticizing the entrepreneurial lifestyle? There had to be a reason why almost everyone I knew was following a different path. The "success track" for college kids pursuing business degrees at that time was super clear:

1. Get an undergraduate degree from a solid four-year university with a good business school, and graduate with honors.

2. Get a couple of years work experience in the corporate world.

3. Go back to school for an MBA at one of the top grad schools.

4. Re-enter the corporate world with your stacked resume, and you're off to the races.

But I must confess... at times during college, I felt as if I was living a double life. Outwardly, I was pursuing the above path, doing and saying all the right things. But inside I knew that the life I truly craved was wildly different.

I stayed on the path, though, and during spring break of my junior year at Syracuse, I traveled west to visit two business schools that were at the top of my list: Stanford and UCLA. I figured that if I was going to continue down this path for now and keep my options open, at least I would do all I could to follow my California dream. It also didn't hurt that these were (and still are) two of the most prestigious MBA programs in the USA.

That's when my story took a surprising twist, and it's probably when Ultimate Vida became inevitable.

> *When was the first time as a teenager or young adult when you felt like you wanted to go in a less popular direction, but felt insecure and/or pressure to follow a more traditional path?*
>
> *How did you navigate that dilemma? Did you go "all in" with your heart and dreams? Did you bury your heart and dreams and do what was "expected?" Did you keep one foot in each of the two doors? Looking back, how do you think these decisions shaped you arriving where you are today? And most importantly, how do you want to handle things going forward?*

Was I the World's First Digital Nomad, or Just an Alien?

When it came time for my trip out west to look at potential MBA programs, I must admit I was fairly hooked on this thing called "The Internet." I put it in quotes because at the time, the internet as we know it barely existed. It was mostly a research and academic tool.

However, there were a few business and marketing "message boards" that I spent a lot of time on. Oh, and I may or may not have also been hooked on chatting with girls online, on services such as AOL, Prodigy & Compuserve (these used to be the "Big 3!").

Anyway, when I planned my trip out west, the idea of being offline for several days or a week felt like lunacy to me. So, I did what anyone in my shoes would have done. I rented a laptop. *Oh wait. There was no one in my shoes.*

I remember looking in the phone book (yes, phone book!) for computer stores in the D.C. area (where my parents lived), and calling around to see if any of them would rent me a laptop. Most of them told me in not so many words that I was crazy. But I finally found one shop – and there was truly only one – who would do it!

Mind you, I had never used a laptop at that point. Few people my age had. High-powered corporate executives were just starting to make use of them. I remember distinctly, though, feeling like taking a laptop with me on that trip was a totally natural and obvious thing to do, despite how rare it was.

So, I went to pick up my laptop rental, and remember it being literally about five times thicker and heavier than the one I'm writing on now. I also remember getting lots of sideways glances at the airport, as I was the only one with a laptop. There was no wifi yet – internet access was only through dial-up (remember that inimitable noise of connecting through dial-up?!) – so at airports and on planes I would just do writing or creative work, and wait until I got to a hotel or someone's apartment to connect on dial-up.

Oh, and speaking of planes? I also remember distinctly pulling out my laptop on that cross-country flight to California, and my seat-mates and the flight attendants looking at me like I was an alien (oh, and the laptop was way too big to fit on my tray table!).

Despite the strange glances, I remember like it was yesterday feeling a rush of excitement every time I pulled out my laptop, innately knowing on some level that this "digital nomad lifestyle" would become the way I lived my life, even though it was a foreign concept at the time. I remember taking an Amtrak train from Los Angeles to Palo Alto (where Stanford is located), and "working" on my laptop as I gazed out the window. I remember imagining myself doing the same thing in Europe, Asia, and all around the world. I felt such a buzz and such a strong sense that I was doing what I was meant to do, even if it hadn't quite taken form yet.

Quick Fast Forward to the Present

I recently spoke at an event for aspiring digital nomads, and the attendees and my fellow speakers affectionately called me the "OG" (which stands for "Original Gangster" and is generally used as a term of endearment or respect for someone who's considered a pioneer or long-time expert in a field). After I gave my presentation and we moved to Q&A, one of the attendees raised his hand and said "So were you the *world's first digital nomad?*"

I must admit, it's a question I had never pondered before. First of all, there's no way to prove it. And second, I wouldn't be so presumptuous as to make that claim.

What I did know beyond the shadow of a doubt was that this was how I wanted to live my life. I felt alive, pulsating with possibility. Like the world was my oyster. Like I was in full control of my destiny. It dawned on me yet again how backwards modern society was in my view. And yet still, the doubts crept in. After all, I was just a young and naïve college kid. And the vast majority of people on the planet with far more experience than me viewed life very differently. Did they know something I didn't? Or was it vice versa? For better or worse, I was way too stubborn to capitulate to the norm or what was "expected." At least not for long...

> *Have you ever done something that was way ahead of its time? Or went completely against the grain of what society or even your own family would have you do? Did you have doubts or insecurities about following this path, even though you just knew in your bones it was the right path for you?*
>
> *What was that inner conflict like for you? What, if anything, would you have done differently? How will you move forward next time you have this kind of inner dilemma?*

The Moment of Truth: Decision Time

College flew by way too fast, and suddenly I found myself in my senior year, and it was Operation Job Search. Recruitment season was in full swing and there were all kinds of job fairs, bulletins, and expos. I felt confused and overwhelmed. On one hand, I felt so clear that I wanted to be in business for myself and craved the freedom lifestyle that no traditional job could give me.

But on the other hand, I still had absolutely no idea what kind of business I could start. And more to the point, how I could start anything that would allow me to fulfill my dream of moving out to California and being able to pay the bills.

I decided to hedge my bets. I made a firm decision that I was going to move to California no matter what. Now, this is where I'd love to tell you I arrived in California with $20 in my pocket and hustled and built an empire. But that's not how it went down. I have a pretty strong tolerance for risk – but not *that* strong. So, I decided that I'd take a mitigated position by only interviewing with California firms, and if I needed to get a job as a stepping stone to get me out to the West Coast, then so be it.

With Syracuse being in the Northeast, naturally firms from Boston and New York City dominated the recruiting scene. Also heavy on the scene were the "Big 6" accounting firms. At this point (in the mid to late 90s), landing a job with one of the Big 6 (now Big 4) accounting firms was considered the entry-level dream job for a college grad majoring in business. Jobs with prestigious consulting firms such as Anderson Consulting (a spinoff of Arthur Anderson accounting firm) were also in high demand. In fact, I remember a buddy of mine who landed a job with Anderson in Boston for $29k/year, and he was over the moon.

This proved to be a bit tricky for me, as California firms did not tend to recruit heavily at Syracuse. There were a few exceptions, however, and I remained persistent. One Los Angeles based consulting firm in particular caught my eye and I called them up and presented myself well and was selected for a phone interview. I must have acquitted myself well in the phone interview, because I was informed that I was a finalist and they wanted to fly me out for an in-person interview! Fly me out?! I'd never been "flown out" anywhere before on any company's dime. I felt important and excited! ☺

The next few weeks were a whirlwind. I flew out. I did the interview. I was rather awed by the prestige of this firm and its address in bustling downtown Los Angeles. I even for a brief moment thought to myself "Hmmm, maybe this corporate thing isn't so bad after all." It would prove to be a short-lived thought. I also took a few days to enjoy all that southern California has to offer, and it only strengthened my resolve to live there — it was where I belonged.

I flew back east to my parents' place, and I'd scarcely been back a few days when I got a call from the firm saying that I got the job! They made me an offer of $34,500. I'll never forget that number. And back then, for a dude right out of college, it wasn't bad at all. I remember in a moment of shallow self-satisfaction, thinking to myself "Wow, they've offered me even more than the Big 6 firms are paying my friends back east." And on top of the salary, they were going to pay my relocation fees! I admit, I kind of felt like a big shot. *It would prove to be short-lived.*

So, I flew out and selected an apartment in beautiful Marina Del Rey. It wasn't right on the beach, but it was within walking distance! And to the world-famous Venice Beach, no less! The moment I signed the lease, I was so freaking excited. I felt like everything was coming together. I was actually going to live in California, right by the beach, just like I'd dreamt about since I was a little boy. And at that moment, it didn't even matter that I'd used the corporate route to make it happen. Little did I know, it soon would matter. *A lot.*

> *Have you ever made a decision that you felt agonizingly conflicted about? A decision that on the surface looked fantastic – so fantastic, that you may have even fooled yourself into thinking it was a good one – but somewhere deep inside, you knew went against everything you actually wanted?*
>
> *How do you remember feeling at the time of that decision? Did you know on some level that it would come back to bite you, but perhaps (like me) were not yet strong enough to confront that? How can you use these types of experiences moving forward to perhaps make a different choice?*

The Sliding Doors of Microsoft

Have you ever seen the moving *Sliding Doors*, with Gwyneth Paltrow? It's one of the most fascinating films I've ever seen.

I won't give away what happens, but I can tell you that the movie is broken into two parts, each beginning with the same scene where she is running to catch a train.

In the first part, she manages to jump on board a split second before the doors slide shut. A certain sequence of events then happens, and her life unfolds in a particular way as a result of getting on that train.

But in the second part, the doors close just before she can make it. A very different set of events ensues, and her life unfolds in a completely different way. All because of the seemingly innocuous event of whether or not she catches that particular train. But was it really innocuous? *Is anything innocuous?*

Anyway, why the heck am I telling you this Sliding Doors story? Well... literally three days after I accepted the job from the firm in Los Angeles and started planning my move out there, I received another phone call... from none other than Microsoft! Informing me that I was a finalist for a marketing position in their product development division, and they wanted to fly me out to Seattle! I politely declined, and informed them that I'd just accepted another position. I didn't think too much of it at the time, other than being kind of wowed by the fact that it was freaking Microsoft. But over the years, I've often pondered that "Sliding Doors" moment in my life, and wondered how my life may have unfolded if I'd started working for Microsoft in the late 90's. Especially in light of the legendary "Microsoft Millionaires" stories of people who jumped on board with the company at that time.

What have been some key "Sliding Doors" moments in your life? While it's fun to ponder what might have been, wistful "what if" thinking isn't really the point here. We'll never be able to anticipate the full "Sliding Doors scenarios" of any decision – such is the magic and mystery of the dance of life.

The takeaway here is to be more conscious and present with our key decisions. No, we can't predict the future, and it's arguable whether we'd even want to. But what we can do is to try to think a few moves ahead and determine the most likely sequence of events that could result from deciding to go in a certain direction.

The "Golden Walls" of Corporate America

By now, you're waiting with bated breath to see how I fared in this prestigious job that I knew in my heart I didn't really want to pursue, right?

Oops, I suppose the existence of this book is a rather glaring spoiler alert, isn't it?!

To cut right to the chase, this turned out to be the only job I ever had in my adult life, and it lasted exactly one year, eight months, and 12 days. But who's counting? Is it weird that I know the exact number of days it lasted, when we're talking about more than 20 years ago?

I'm not gonna say it was all bad. I had an "interesting" honeymoon period that lasted... oh, *five days*. Here's how it went down...

My dad took me shopping for suits and ties and I felt so stylish and grown up. Memories of those dapper business travelers whom I was in awe of as a child rushed back.

I flew out to California once again on the firm's dime (they also paid my relocation fee), and re-acquainted myself with the apartment I had selected in beautiful Marina Del Rey – in walking distance from the beach! My coastal lifestyle was taking shape! Things were falling into place. So much so, that I temporarily ignored the blindingly obvious fact that deep down inside, I knew the corporate world was not for me.

When my alarm went off at 6:17 AM on my first day of work, it was one of the few times in my life an alarm has ever excited me. I was running on pure adrenaline, ready to take on the world. Incidentally, it was also the only time that fighting L.A. rush hour traffic felt "cool."

I pulled up to 520 South Grand Avenue, beneath the Biltmore Hotel in downtown Los Angeles, looking like a million bucks (if I do say so myself!) in my navy blue suit, crisp white dress shirt, and purple silk tie. I went through orientation and met the partners of the firm, several of whom were considered legends in the litigation consulting field. One of them even testified in the O.J. Simpson trial! Entry level people like me (we were called "Analysts") crunched the numbers and prepared them for trial. I'll admit, for a brief moment, I thought to myself "Wow, I've really made it. This is what success looks like. Maybe I can actually do this."

My second day, I was still riding high, although the alarm wasn't quite so pleasant this time. But I still felt important. I still felt accomplished. From the outside, this Syracuse grad working for an esteemed consulting firm in Los Angeles was the picture of a young man destined for success.

My third day, I went to lunch with a few of the Associates (next level up), and that's when the luster began to wear off. They regaled me with tales of working 14-hour days, as if it were a badge of honor. They explained to me how to climb the ranks of the firm, from Junior Analyst to Senior Analyst to Junior Associate to Senior Associate to Partner to Senior Partner. They talked about how badly they hoped to earn a five percent raise that year. Five percent? Really??

I remember laughing at their jokes and feigning enthusiasm at their lofty corporate aspirations while silently starting to question what the hell I had gotten myself into. I started to wonder what was wrong with me. Why was I not enamored by climbing this prestigious corporate ladder like my fellow Junior Analysts?

By my fourth day, the shine was firmly wearing off, and as the alarm went off that day, I felt a tense, uncomfortable energy. But I gamely pulled on my suit, hopped in my car, and vowed to make the most of this rapidly worrisome situation as I battled the rush hour traffic. I told myself, "At least it's Friday and the weekend's almost here."

Upon my arrival that day, the entire firm was summoned into the conference room for an emergency meeting. We were notified that there had been a key development in the trial that one of our major clients was involved in, and it was "all hands on deck" for the weekend. I didn't really know what that meant, so I asked one of the second year Analysts, and he said "Yeah, man, that's pretty normal. You'll love it. It's exciting!"

Say *what*?! How is working weekends "normal" when I'm already working long hours during the week? And surely if I work weekends or into the evening, there would be some overtime pay, right? Negative. I was on a fixed salary. I remember wondering to myself how is it that manual labor employees earn overtime, while "rising corporate stars" with business degrees just work crazy hours with no additional compensation? Was I weird for questioning such things? No one else seemed to be asking!

When my alarm went off on Day Five (Saturday morning, I might add), the honeymoon period was firmly over. In fact, I distinctly remember breaking into a cold sweat. I had made plans for a great first weekend by the beach, and suddenly I had to spend all day in a windowless conference room in a downtown office, poring through legal documents and making spreadsheet entries.

So, there you have it. Exactly five days into my corporate career, I realized with a visceral certainty that I can't even put into words that this life was not for me. Mind you, I never showed it. Not once. On the outside, I was a dedicated team player, putting in the long days and weekends. I laughed at everyone's jokes, and even told a few myself.

But inside, it wasn't such a pretty picture. I felt lost and insecure. I secretly wondered what was wrong with me. Why did I have such an intense negative reaction to a job and professional situation that others my age craved? On the outside, I was the very picture of professional success – a rising star. And yet on the inside, I wasn't even one week in, and I felt like I was living a lie. Part of me wondered "Why can't I be more normal?"

It wasn't the first time I'd asked myself that question, nor would it be the last.

Ultimately, the voice inside my head screaming "get out" and "be free" was just too intense. I knew what I had to do. But I had to be strategic about it.

What was your "tipping point" when you knew beyond the shadow of a doubt that your current life wasn't (or isn't!) working for you?

I know it might be painful to take yourself back there (or be fully present to it if it's happening right now), but it's crucial that you do. Because only by facing reality and being brutally honest with yourself can you begin to chart a new course.

Escape From the Golden Walls

I vividly remember that first "work weekend" experience. It finally wrapped up around 9 pm on Sunday. Outwardly, I was a convivial trooper, exchanging high fives with my office mates – a dutiful team player who'd done his part to carry out the mission.

But as I drove home, I was shaken. I knew with absolute certainty that I didn't want this to be my life. I felt it with every fiber of my being. But I also knew that I couldn't just walk away tomorrow or the next day, as it would leave me with no money and nowhere to go. Plus, just getting any old random job wasn't going to cut it if I wanted to stay in Marina Del Rey by the beach. Which was the whole point of moving out to California.

So, I resolved to plan my escape, but to be strategic about it. And when I set the dreaded alarm for 6:17 the following morning, I knew that I had to get a plan in place.

My Double Life

Starting the next day at work, I began to channel my inner James Bond. I considered myself a "Double Agent" of sorts. Outwardly, I was a good company man, carrying out whatever work was assigned to me. But in my downtime, rather than shooting the shit with my co-workers or reading the sports section of the L.A. Times, I would voraciously scour the internet for ideas and opportunities.

Now let me back up a minute here and define "Scour the internet." This was circa 1997. The "dot-com bubble" was still in its infancy. E-commerce barely existed. Social media was still years away (Facebook was still almost a decade from inception!). Google existed, but was a smaller, almost "fringe" search engine at that time. The biggest search engine around was... drumroll please... Alta Vista! I know, right?

Anyway, I decided to revisit the direct marketing obsession that had been a central theme during high school and college, and see what kind of opportunities I could find on the world wide web. There were no "blogs" at this point, but forums and message boards were just starting to emerge. As were online newsletters, known at the time as "e-zines." I began reading everything I could get my hands (or should I say eyeballs) on. I would often do this surreptitiously at my cubicle between carrying out various tasks for the firm.

My "Empire" Started at... a Public Library?

But where I really started gathering momentum was during my lunch hour, where I'd visit the L.A. Public Library, conveniently located only a block away! To this day, the L.A. Library remains one of the best around. If the clerks in the business section didn't know me by name, they certainly knew my face!

At the library, I concentrated my time and energy in two areas:

First, I dove further and further down this rapidly emerging rabbit hole known as the internet (on the library computers, with no one looking over my shoulder!). It was like the wild west, and each day was a new discovery. I'd pore through posts and threads on the few "online marketing message boards" that existed at that time. I'd sign up for "e-zines" on marketing and business, which were quite a novelty at that time. E-commerce and "shopping carts" didn't quite exist yet in their current form, PayPal had not yet been founded, yet people were still figuring out clever ways to make money online. I was hooked.

The second thing I did was double down on my fascination with direct marketing. During high school and college, I'd study ads and promotions and try to reverse engineer them and understand the psychology behind them. But somehow, I never read a single book about business or marketing. Crazy, huh? I decided to change that. And fast. I was at one of the finest libraries in the world, after all! I began to read classic marketing works by luminaries like Eugene Schwartz, Claude Hopkins, Joe Sugarman, Dan Kennedy, and Jay Abraham. From these works, I gained a more solid and grounded understanding of the psychology that goes into creating an offer and capturing people's attention.

Spam Baby, Spam

During this time, there was another movement bubbling beneath the surface and quietly taking shape. No one likes to talk about it now, as it's been illegal for quite some time, but the trend I'm referring to is spam. Back then, it was simply called "bulk email" and was perfectly legal. It didn't take a genius to see the power and potential rewards of blasting out a promotional email to thousands or even millions. But the rub was that the proper systems and infrastructure to actually sell something and take orders from these mass emails was sorely lacking.

However, as you might imagine, young Jedi Jesse had other ideas about how to deploy this "bulk email" thing. Remember AOL? OK, maybe not. But I'm guessing you've at least heard about it? For a brief time there, that robotic voice exclaiming "You've got mail!" upon sign-in was quite a thrilling experience. So much so that it became somewhat of a cultural phenomenon, and even became the title of a movie starring Tom Hanks and Meg Ryan.

Anyway, AOL had a "member directory" in which people could share as much or little about themselves as they chose – including their job title and/ or business! BOOM! Another light bulb moment. I remembered that I had recently seen an ad for an "extractor" software that would spider lists or directories and pull out the email addresses or screen names. It sounded interesting, but I couldn't see quite how I would use it at the time, so I mentally filed it away and moved on. But now it was all coming together.

In a matter of days, I:

- Purchased this extractor software, funded by good 'ol Corporate America, in what most of the world (including those closest to me) would've no doubt regarded as another "foolish bizopp scheme."
- Used the software to extract relevant AOL screen names that had terms such as "CEO" or "Director of Marketing" in their member directory profile.
- Blasted out an email to a bunch of members — can't remember if it was hundreds or thousands, but it was a lot — offering a "free website analysis." (Interesting to note that even then, I was taking a service mentality: How can I help and what can I offer? It would prove to be a philosophy that served me very well, and became the basis for everything I did, including this book! In the pages and chapters that follow, we'll look at how YOU can use it for your own purposes, and help people in the process!)

'Twas the Night Before Inbox Explosion

I remember I clicked "send" on that message late at night and then tried to sleep, as I knew my alarm would go off in a few short hours for my day job. But sleep was just not happening. I was too anxious and excited about the email I had blasted out. Would I get any responses? Was I even qualified to give a website analysis? What would I say? How could I help these people? What might it lead to?

I finally drifted off to sleep at around 3 am, and was cruelly awakened by that blaring alarm (which was now officially my most dreaded sound in the world) only three hours and 17 minutes later. I immediately stumbled to my computer in a bleary-eyed stupor, and signed onto AOL (this is all on dialup Internet, mind you), hoping against hope that I'd hear those three magic words, "You've got mail," because it would likely mean that I'd gotten at least one response to my message.

What happened next completely floored me and left me aghast. My inbox was *flooded* with requests for the free website analysis. I'm talking dozens, if not hundreds of responses. And they continued pouring in by the minute.

I quickly showered and reluctantly donned my suit and tie as I tried to process what was happening. And on my way out the door, I checked my email one last time to find that another 20 or so replies had rolled in while I was getting ready for work!

As I slogged through the rush hour traffic, a rush of emotions burned a hole in my head. The excitement of the flood of responses and the feeling that I was really onto something. The panic and overwhelm of trying to figure out how the heck I'd actually deliver so many website analyses with any degree of quality. The self-doubt creeping in, questioning whether I was even qualified to do those website analyses.

Operation Website Analysis

But as I plodded through another day at the office, feigning interest in my work, I managed to re-center myself and get excited all over again about the flood of replies to my email. And when I got home that evening, I made a pot of coffee (back then, I used to drink coffee at all hours – even the night!) and got to it. I felt my confidence surging back as I realized that I had three key factors working my favor:

1. Back then, almost every website royally sucked and was basically an electronic version of a company brochure. (Key point: it's way easier to look like a genius in a pool of incompetency!)

2. While nowadays, "free offers" are a dime a dozen, back then it was rather avant garde to offer anything for free, much less something with as high a perceived value as a website analysis (Key point: all offers of help are <u>not</u> created equal! What could you theoretically offer that is unique and/or has a high perceived value? For now, just answer this question and don't even think about making money!)

3. Once I calmed the self-doubting voice inside my head, I realized that even though I was a recent college grad and was about to correspond with CEOs and Directors of Marketing, the reality was that I very likely knew far more than they did about direct marketing and the psychology of what makes people buy. That particular skill has very little to do with age or formal education. (Key point: in what areas do you naturally know more than 95% of all people, whether through experience, natural ability, or both? Focus your efforts in that direction and watch what happens!)

When in Doubt, Always "B.O.S.S."

We're going to take a majestic and inspiring deep dive into service in the chapters that follow (complete with 3D glasses!), so I don't want to steal our thunder too much here. But let me give you a sneak preview by revealing one of the foremost core concepts that will serve you well in business, in life, and in your Ultimate Vida.

B.O.S.S. = Be Of Supreme Service

So when in doubt, B.O.S.S.! *Always* B.O.S.S.

Between that night and the next few days, I must've delivered over 100 website analyses! It was intense. So, I went back to the basics, and B.O.S.S.'d it up big time!

Here are the key points of what made these analyses work, that you can adapt to whatever you end up doing. (Don't worry, I'll help you figure it out in the coming chapters.) ☺ :

1. I didn't half-ass it. I went all in and went the extra mile. I really took time to understand their business and who they were as individuals as best I could, which allowed me to make my content and delivery very personal.

2. I gave meaty, actionable tips that they could use and benefit from, whether we ended up working together or not. People often have better instincts than we give them credit for. When we "tease" or hold back our best stuff, they can sniff that out and we lose credibility. Treat 'em like you would your best friends & family, and you'll be amazed at what they'll be willing to do with you (including paying you handsomely)!

3. I included a light call to action that was very low key and non-salesy. I let the substance of my work speak for itself. I simply said that if they found my analysis useful and want to discuss in more detail how I can help them implement these tips and strategies, to reach out by phone or email.

Key point here is the word **implement**. Now more than ever, information is a dime a dozen. You can get instructions on how to do just about anything via Google or YouTube. Implementation, on the other hand, is king and is worth its weight in gold. If you are able to not just tell people how to get a result, but actually get the result for or with them, you will be in higher demand than you can even imagine.

Additional note: when I originally did this, I limited my offer to business owners in southern California. Back then, online marketing was still in its infancy, and my instinct was that people would feel more comfortable working with someone they could actually meet with face to face. It proved to be a good decision. Nowadays it's not as crucial, as it's commonplace to work with people via email, Skype, Zoom, Facebook, etc. But even in today's day and age, don't underestimate the timeless power of in-person interaction. Getting face-to-face is and always will be more powerful than any technology!

Anyway, from these analyses, I received a couple dozen calls and emails – seven of which led to face-to-face meetings. And from these seven meetings, I landed my first three clients!

- A dance and production company in Santa Monica
- A real estate investment firm in Orange County
- A motivational speaker in San Diego

When $250 Felt Like $1 Million…

I'll never forget, for as long as I live, the moment when I landed my very first client (the Santa Monica production company). Michelle (their CEO) handed me a check for $250, and it may as well have been $1 Million, because that's what it felt like! I was on Cloud Nine.

The sense of validation and possibility was simply amazing. I felt chills running through me as I realized the enormity of what had just happened: I thought of an idea, executed and promoted it electronically with no real costs, and discovered that people were willing to pay me money for a skill that I privately wondered if I was truly qualified to deliver. I was speechless, and made an inner vow to blow away these three clients (and all future ones) by overdelivering like they'd never seen before.

…And Gave Me the Confidence to Officially Leave My Job!

Now, this is where I'd love to tell you that I marched into my boss's office the next day and dramatically said "I quit!"

But that's not how it went down. Dramatic outbursts aren't really my style. Plus, the high-stakes drama had already played out in my mind and in my heart when I decided five days into my job (more than a year earlier!) that the corporate world was definitely *not* for me. I remember distinctly feeling that it was a decision that was both terrifying and obvious.

But once the decision was made? I learned an extremely powerful lesson: If you have a firm conviction in your mind and heart about what's right for you? This conviction will become your very fuel for making the uncomfortable comfortable; for creating and living a life so extraordinary that you'll have to pinch yourself to remind yourself it's real.

With my job (called an "Analyst"), it was understood that it was roughly a two-year run, at which time we'd either try for a promotion within the firm, or step down and apply to business school where we'd re-enter the work force two years later armed with an MBA from a prestigious university. Of the seven analysts from my recruiting class, I was the only one who did neither. Shocking, right?

There was a further tacit understanding that we'd have roughly a three-month window around that two-year mark to officially leave our position. You'll be equally non-shocked to know that my end date just "happened" to fall before any of the other Analysts.

Making My Escape Official

So, now this was a real thing. I was officially leaving the firm. My last day was May 15, 1998. I had an intense mix of fear and excitement around this. But I also had a deep certainty that it was the right move – indeed the *only* move that stood a chance of leading me to the kind of life I wanted.

Almost immediately after making the decision, a fascinating pattern started to emerge. I noticed my fear decreasing and my excitement increasing, by the day; even by the minute. It's not that I had suddenly figured out all the answers or worked out how I was going to support myself. It's that I knew with a visceral certainty that the life I was about to leave behind was decidedly *not* for me, and the one I was moving towards was the only one that fit in with my vision.

Suddenly, the day was upon me. I remember it like it was yesterday. My last day fell on a Friday, and I was dressed in a plaid button-down shirt and blue jeans (Fridays were casual days at the office!). I found it quite fitting that rather than putting on a suit and tie, I'd be dressing for my new life! And for the first time since my first few days of work, the rush hour traffic didn't bother me. In fact, I was bursting with excitement knowing this was the last time I'd have to deal with it and that my time was about to become my own.

The day itself was a blur. I didn't get much actual work done, as it was really about closing out my affairs with the firm. I said my goodbyes to my co-workers, and at the end of the day, walked out the doors of 520 South Grand Avenue, for the final time. I had a celebratory drink at the corner bar down the street with a couple of my co-workers (or as of a few minutes earlier, *ex* co-workers!), and was positively giddy. None of them really understood what I was going to do next – I can't blame them; I didn't fully know myself – but I had absolute clarity that I was making the right move, and it felt amazing.

To this day, every year on May 15, I celebrate my "Freedom Anniversary." It has become my most treasured and sacred day of the year. Two years ago, on May 15, 2018, I had the urge to come full circle, so I drove into downtown LA and walked by my old stomping grounds. Here I am, in front of the very building that I walked out of 20 years earlier to begin my UltimateVida...

Looking back, I can say that I definitely benefited from a healthy dose of stubbornness and luck. But I can also say that I had by far the most crucial ingredient in place – that unmistakable certainty that I was doing the right thing.

Why should this matter to you?

You may not realize it yet (though hopefully you do!), but you've got a stunningly powerful, unstoppable force taking shape. It's in your mind, your heart, and indeed your **hands**, right in this moment.

Now, if I'm going to make an assertion that bold, you deserve for it to be backed up before I continue. So, it goes like this. The title and/or description of this book – whose premise is how to leave your job and design the life of your dreams — sufficiently compelled you to acquire it and read it up to this point.

That shows serious guts and strength of conviction.

I dare say, it shows you've got a clarity for your life's vision just as strong as I had twenty-plus years ago.

But now we're going to take your courageous conviction and add something extraordinarily powerful to the mix. Something I would've given just about anything for back when I was in your position. Something that would've saved me years of time and hundreds of thousands of dollars testing different things and trying to figure out what worked.

You're about to learn the methodology for how to make it happen, and get an actual road map to follow! I searched the world high and low for this treasure map back in the day. In libraries, bookstores, the early days of the Internet, talking to other entrepreneurs — you name it. I tried everything I could think of. But there was just no proven path to follow. Thus, I stumbled around and tried a bit of this, a bit of that, until I arrived upon, tested and refined the formula I'm about to share with you.

The Hidden Dangers of Coasting and Avoidance

Now, I'm not going to glorify or romanticize my early days in business and say "the rest is history." Eventually, the high of those first three clients wore off and I realized that it would take not just periodic bursts of motivation and activity, but consistent and strategic execution to build anything resembling a sustainable business. (The way to do that is to "B.O.S.S. it up" with 3D Glasses – more on that very soon!).

Oh, and if you're wondering whether I was financially stable when I left my job? The answer is a resounding NO. I had a few thousand dollars in savings from high school and college. And I had managed to put aside a few hundred dollars per month from my paycheck while I had my job. As you can imagine, this amount of money was only enough to last me a few months at best living by the beach in southern California.

Given my less than stable position, you might assume that I lined up a part-time job to support myself while I continued to pursue my Internet lifestyle dream. But if you assumed that, you'd be wrong. I wasn't nearly so sensible. I decided to go "all in" on making my Ultimate Vida a reality.

Was this foolish or naïve on my part? Probably. But if I had to do it all over again? I'd do the exact same thing. And I'm not just saying that because things eventually worked out. In fact, I think things eventually worked out precisely *because* I went all in.

Now, by no means am I saying you need to make the same decision I did. I can't possibly know all the variables at play in your life. This is a deeply personal decision that is yours and yours alone. More on that in a few minutes.

What I do strongly suggest, however, is that you validate that you're able to earn some amount of money from your new business, even if it's a very small amount. Spoiler alert: I'll show you exactly how to do that, step by step, in this very book. ☺

Was $250 enough for me to live on? Not even close. But as I explained earlier, to me it felt like a million dollars. Why? Because I had identified a problem that people urgently wanted to solve and were willing to pay for. And I had already "tested the waters" and discovered that there were a lot more business owners just like the one who paid me $250 who had similar problems I could solve. That's what gave me the (irrational?) courage to talk myself into going "all in."

> *It took me a good two years before my new Internet business was producing at a level where I felt a modicum of financial security.*

There were some stressful times during those two years for sure – including a few where I silently wondered if I'd make it – but I just knew so clearly that there was no turning back, and that I could never be happy living a conventional life. So, I kept charging forward, perhaps stubbornly and naively, but charging forward nonetheless.

In the years that followed, I tackled business on the Internet from just about every angle you can imagine:

- I ran companies and had employees
- I went virtual with subcontractors only
- I consulted for other companies
- I bought and sold online businesses (I call this "digital real estate")
- I coached other aspiring marketers
- I did affiliate marketing (selling other people's products and services for a commission)

I feel like I am an "Internet cat" who has at *least* nine lives (and probably a lot more!) doing online business.

During this time, some of my projects were successful, and others not as much, but thankfully I was always able to produce enough revenues to pay the bills and live a nice lifestyle.

If I had to boil it down to one key factor, though? The one crucial move that allowed me to go from receiving periodic checks for $250 or a bit more, to building a real and sustainable business?

It was listening to my audience and giving them what they wanted.

I've put that last sentence in bold and italics because it is literally the key to your jailbreak and unlocking your Ultimate Vida. And it's what the upcoming sections of this book will show you exactly how to do (Don't worry, I know you probably don't have an audience quite yet – I'll show you how to find and build one, too). ☺

In my case, it went like this...

After I started offering those free website analyses?

I made a classic and costly mistake that would prove to cost me significant time and money: I tried to be all things to all people. I foolishly assumed that if business owners liked my site analyses, it would suddenly qualify me to design their site, market their site, set up their hosting and merchant account, and essentially be their "one stop shop" for all their Internet solutions.

Looking back, it seems laughably absurd that I actually thought I could deliver all these services. But what can I say... I was young and ambitious, and maybe I let my early success make me a bit too cocky. So, this mistake left me in a bit of a holding pattern for a year or so. Where I was making just enough to get by, but never enough to get ahead – probably because my clients were rightfully confused about what my specialty was and how we could keep working together after they initially hired me based on the site analysis.

But during that year, an interesting trend started to emerge. One that I should've picked up on sooner, but thankfully I eventually clued in and acted on it. I started to notice that by far the most common and urgent request I was getting was for search engine optimization (SEO). In other words, helping my clients be found on the first page or two of the major search engines. At that time, Google was NOT the leading engine. But Yahoo was on the scene. As were plenty of now defunct or irrelevant engines like Lycos and Altavista. The key point, though, was that in the late 90's, one of the most burning desires for business owners online was to be found by the search engines!

So, I resolved to "Give 'em what they wanted!" Back then, SEO was seen as a fairly technical skill. And I was most certainly *not* technical. But I'd figured out by now that the key to earning people's trust and selling any product or service is always about communication and marketing. So, I set out to learn all I could about SEO – not from a technical standpoint, but in terms of how it could transform a business and therefore transform the business owner's life. I wrote a sales letter to promote our SEO services (Don't worry, you won't have to do this – I did things the hard way).

And for a change, I made an intelligent decision. I realized that I was not going to suddenly become an SEO expert. So, I researched existing SEO firms (there weren't too many of them back then!) to try and find one to partner with. After a bit of due diligence via phone and email, I found a firm in Portland who resonated with me. So, I flew up to meet with them and we struck an informal arrangement where I would market SEO packages to business owners, they'd deliver the service, and we'd share the revenues.

Mind you, I had no SEO customers at this stage. But I had a clear demand for these services, and I'd already written a sales letter. So, I was (naively?) confident that I'd be able to bring in lots of business. Plus, the Portland firm really had nothing to lose. They'd get clients delivered to them with no risk. So, I flew back to Los Angeles with an SEO partnership under my belt.

I then wrote an article which was called "The Naked Truth About Search Engine Optimization." It took the angle that at its core, SEO is not about "meta tags" or anything technical, but rather having a clearly defined MDA (Most Desired Action – I believe I coined that term!).

I submitted it to every online publication geared towards business owners that I could find. Most publications, I never heard back from. A few ran it, but had very small readerships.

But finally, I hit the jackpot and had a major breakthrough moment. One that reminded me of my inbox explosion from my "AOL spam" experiment. A major online publication picked up my article and blasted it out to their list of tens of thousands of business owners!

I closed more business in the first week of that article hitting than I had in the previous year of barely getting by! I scrambled night and day to fulfill the orders; meaning on my end communicating with the clients; and on the Portland firm's end, actually do the SEO! Looking back, I'd say we did a decent job. But the truth is, I was in a bit over my head. I'd never had anywhere near this many clients.

After a few months, though, it became clear that the Portland firm and I had different visions about this business. So, we amicably parted ways. My immediate priority, of course, then became finding a replacement. This time, I wanted someone in-house rather than partnering with another firm. And for the first time in my life, I had the funds available to hire someone! So, I flew up to Spokane, Washington to meet with a woman who'd found me online and reached out a while back. It turned out to be a perfect match, as she was looking to leave her full-time job and wanted to work remotely. So, we came to an agreement, and she ended up doing SEO for us for many years to come!

On the surface, I had things rolling and some of my friends in the industry (and outside as well) would tell me that I had the "Midas touch." And while I was grateful for their compliments, I also distinctly remember thinking to myself "How long can this run last? Don't most entrepreneurs hit rock bottom at some point?"

It would prove to be eerie foreshadowing.

My Invisible Crisis

It's painful to be this brutally honest with myself, but the truth is I reached a point somewhere along the way where I grew a bit restless and complacent. I cherished my freedom lifestyle, and the vehicle to achieve it, which was

Internet marketing. But I remember thinking to myself, "There's got to be more." I think, looking back, the reason I felt this way is because I was focusing so heavily on my business and not addressing my personal life. *It would prove to be a costly mistake.*

I remember thinking to myself, "How can I possibly feel bored or restless? This is the life I always dreamed of!" But I couldn't escape the growing inner turmoil, hard as I tried to block it out.

I reached an existential crisis of sorts – like I referred to in the intro of this book. I don't know if it was burnout or emptiness that I felt – probably a combination of both. While things looked great from the outside, they weren't so pretty on the inside.

That's when I started going in completely different directions. I significantly increased the amount that I traveled. And I started doing some international real estate investing as well. I knew nothing about real estate, but I had a partner who was an expert, and I felt like I wanted to do something new.

Looking back, it's now acutely and painfully clear why things got off track, and ultimately spiraled out of control.

Deep breath... time to fast forward a bit, and let you in deeper... *way* deeper. Into the searing pain I got myself into. This is NOT easy for me, but it's got to be done, and I'd be doing you a MAJOR disservice if I left this part out. Here goes:

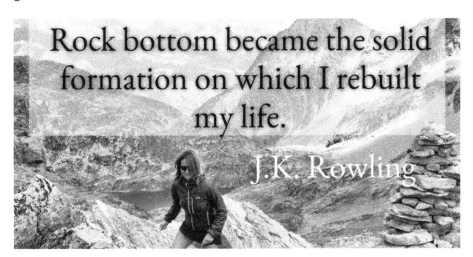

Rock bottom became the solid formation on which I rebuilt my life.

J.K. Rowling

The common refrain when we get knocked down or hit rock bottom is, "It brought me to my knees."

The Art of Freedom

In my case, it brought me to my ass.

Literally.

Naked, in my shower.

I had completely hit rock bottom.

I sobbed uncontrollably, until the cascading water was indistinguishable from my tears.

Under my ass was a filthy, moldy tub.

I'm talking unsanitary.

I'd never bathed in such conditions before, as a child nor an adult.

The thing was, I just didn't care.

My sense of pride and self-worth – my fight – had been stripped bare.

My marriage was breaking down.

My dad's health was breaking down.

I had zero ability to focus on work, so my business was breaking down.

And my business was the one part of my life where I'd always been successful even when I had other issues.

So, in a very large sense, I felt like my entire identity and life as I knew it was breaking down.

Looking back, it's easy to connect the dots, heartbreaking as they were...

Why should the surfaces in my house be any cleaner than my stained, shattered soul?

If anything, the tub looked sparkling compared to what I felt inside.

Why am I sharing all this with you right now, you may ask?

Why have I suddenly shifted gears and started this "rock bottom" story in what's otherwise hopefully an inspiring and game-changing roadmap for you?

It's definitely not for fun – I can tell you that much.

I'm actually terrified right now. My fingers are trembling, and my heart is racing as I write this.

I wrote much of this book in coffee shops, planes, airports and hotels. But this part, I knew I needed to stay home and be alone.

Because I knew I'd have frequent breakdowns. I knew I'd start sobbing uncontrollably again.

And for the first time in my life, that's ok.

You see, I spent most of my life blocking out pain, and I didn't even know it.

And when the pain got to be too much?

I'd suffer in silence. I'd pretend that everything was ok.

I think on some level, I felt ashamed of being in pain because on the surface, I had the life that everyone wanted.

Freedom, travel, marriage, being my own boss. The whole nine yards.

So, I think in some twisted way, I felt like I "had no right" to feel pain or be upset because I lived this "charmed life."

But that's utter nonsense, if you think about it. I mean, look how many rich and famous people in the entertainment industry commit suicide, overdose, or are miserable. And their lives are way more "charmed" than mine ever was.

I came to realize that once our basic survival needs are met, our external circumstances have little, if anything, to do with our happiness or inner state.

I think I also felt guilty on some level for feeling so low, when I knew that so many others were battling situations far more dire and heartbreaking than mine.

Just last week I had dinner with a truly beautiful woman on the inside and out who is a widow at age 36. I listened intently and held the space for her as she told me the story of her husband's passing, allowing herself to feel every last morsel of what she said. It was one of the most breathtaking displays of vulnerability I've ever witnessed.

I've met others like her who have endured unspeakable tragedies.

And beyond tragedy, let's remember that over 92% of the world population breathes substandard air, according to the World Health Organization.

Let's also remember that almost half the world – over 3 billion people – live on less than $2.50 per day.

It would serve us well to always remember that if we wake up breathing clean air with a roof over our heads and food in the fridge, we are blessed beyond belief.

So, I'd somehow feel guilty or ashamed of how intense my darkest moments felt, because I told myself that they were nothing compared to others' plights.

This turned into a vicious cycle where I'd not only feel down and anxious about what I was going through, but I'd beat myself up because I didn't think I had a "right" to feel it.

Remember how I joked that my independence and stubbornness started in the womb when I was born late?

It served me well in many respects. I seriously doubt I would've started my own business or achieved the freedom lifestyle without it.

But it had a darker side too – at least for me.

When I was going through my darkest period...

The sadness often unbearable...

Sometimes literally trembling in fear...

My own life suddenly unrecognizable to me...

The resilience, resourcefulness, and rock solid "mental game" that I'd always been able to summon, maddeningly absent when I needed it most...

On some level, I knew I wasn't going to get out of this alone.

And yet, I didn't reach out for help, either.

Looking back, I don't think I even knew how.

I'd never had to.

I was always the guy helping people, not asking for help.

Until it became too much.

Until that day when I sat naked on my ass in my shower, sobbing uncontrollably.

At that moment, I was honestly scared for my life. I didn't know what could happen. I felt completely out of control.

So, I finally reached out for help.

Little by little, I began opening up to my family and close friends about what I was going through.

For the first time in my life, I got a therapist.

And for all my sessions with her?

There's one moment that stands out and to this day jolts me to the core.

One time I was sitting on her couch and being particularly hard on myself.

Beating myself up for getting in such a funk and not being able to work my way out as quickly as I wanted or hoped for.

And as I was going off on myself, she suddenly raised her voice (she had never done that before) and said...

"STOP. Just STOP. Would you EVER treat a friend or family member the way you're treating yourself right now?"

Her words shook me to the core and I will never forget them.

They served as the "permission slip" for me to start digging myself out of this hole.

Step by step, piece by piece.

And the past few years I've quietly chipped away at my issues and challenges.

Not to become perfect or invincible. That will never happen.

But to become whole again.

To get to a place of self-love.

Where I can look at myself in the mirror and be proud of who I am.

Because that's the level I wanted to reach before releasing Ultimate Vida to the world and asking to be trusted as a leader.

I am sobbing again as I write this.

I can literally feel the cold, wet tiles of the shower on my ass even though I'm sitting on a plush couch right now.

And for the first time in my life, I'm ok with taking myself back there.

I spent my whole life trying to block out the "bad stuff" without even realizing it.

But what is "bad," really?

Had that "bad" period never happened...

As dark and terrifying as it was...

I never would've arrived at where I am today.

Which, don't get me wrong, is still a work in progress. And always will be.

But I feel more open than ever.

More vulnerable than ever.

More comfortable in my own skin than ever.

More present than ever.

More *alive* than ever.

Would this book have been written had I not gone through all that?

I don't know. Maybe.

The strategies and tactics still would've been useful.

But they would have had no soul behind them.

No essence.

No *life*.

And I firmly believe they would've made far less of an impact on you.

Because it is this, my friend, that is the Ultimate Vida.

This is the real stuff.

Don't get me wrong – the strategies and tactics I teach in this book are extremely powerful.

If you apply them and are consistent with them, you'll likely have success, no matter what's going on in your life.

So why, then, am I even including this chapter?

Well, because it's actually the most important one of all.

Because there is no strategy or tactic in the world that will set you free more than facing yourself.

So, if you want to achieve a specific goal or up front target like leaving your job and starting to build a business and your freedom lifestyle?

Follow the steps in this book, be consistent, and you can absolutely get there.

But if you want to sustain it?

Make sure you're at peace with yourself.

Truly at peace.

And if you're not?

That's so ok.

That's more than ok.

But please – oh please – do not try to face your demons alone.

I don't care how much you've been through or how strong you are.

Demons are not meant to be faced alone.

That's why as I sit here writing this chapter through tears and Kleenex, I can say that it is the privilege and honor of my lifetime to say that I've got your back.

We've got your back.

The **Ultimate Vida family** has got your back.

We are all one.

One love.

One journey.

One extended family.

One Ultimate Vida.

Let's do this!

The Lesson I Learned From Hitting Rock Bottom

You might be thinking, "Wait a minute. How did he suddenly go from living this charmed life to hitting rock bottom? Surely he must be leaving something out?"

No, I'm really not. And that's kind of the whole point, and the whole problem. For so many years, I would just block out anything even remotely resembling pain. I would do this so instinctively that it would just happen on auto-pilot, without me making a conscious decision to do so.

But what I've learned since then – not just from my own rock-bottom, but from reading, studying and my therapy – is this irrefutable fact and equation:

"What goes in MUST come out."

I cannot possibly stress that fact enough. And make no mistake – it IS a fact.

Sounds kind of obvious, right? But here's the kicker, which is far less obvious, but incredibly destructive:

If you do what I did, and practice avoidance as a coping mechanism? What "comes out" will do so with a force that's exponentially more intense than it would have been had you dealt with things as they came up.

Nowadays, when tough situations come up – including very painful ones – I actually embrace them. I won't pretend I'm always evolved enough to be thankful they're happening, as certain things really suck in the moment they're happening. But I'm always conscious to not deny any emotion that I have. To give whatever I'm feeling its place at the table, whether it's good, bad or ugly.

In a moment, we'll be switching gears completely from my story into the nuts and bolts of how to build your Ultimate Vida. I'm about to share with you some seriously powerful and valuable stuff! But before I do, I urge you to take a moment to pause and reflect on my "rock-bottom" reveal, and ask yourself how YOU deal with painful or difficult situations. Because, crazy as it may sound? I promise you that letting pain in and not practicing avoidance, will be as powerful as anything else I'll be sharing with you in this book...

With that said, let's rock and roll! ☺

When to Make *Your* Escape

Time to switch gears here from my story to yours. And more specifically, how to navigate the crossroads and defining moment that almost every budding entrepreneur inevitably faces in the early days: When to make the leap and go "all in" with your entrepreneurial ventures. Put another way, when to stop relying on a paycheck and commit to creating your own paycheck.

That's obviously a very personal decision that neither I, nor even those closest to you, are qualified to make for you.

It's your decision — and yours alone.

That said, here's my two cents on the framework for making this key decision. Basically, there are two schools of thought. Consider a spectrum from most risky to least risky, in terms of when to make the leap.

The "most risky" end of the spectrum would say that if you know you want to be an entrepreneur, go all in immediately. That there will never be a better moment than right now. And there's a lot to be said for that. After all, life is extremely fragile and unpredictable, and tomorrow is never guaranteed. Energetically, there's something very powerful about fully committing right here and right now to the direction that you know you want to go.

The other end of the spectrum – the "least risky" end – says to wait until you manage to replace your income from your day job with your side business, and then and only then, make the leap. This viewpoint also has its merit. Especially if you have a family to support and/or have low risk tolerance (although keep in mind that if you're reading this book, it's almost certain by definition that you have a higher than average risk tolerance).

The Key Point: It All Starts Now

Most importantly, please take the following key point to heart: whether you make the leap tomorrow, next week, next month, or next year... if you are EVER going to reach your Ultimate Vida, your new freedom lifestyle MUST begin in your mind and in your heart *right now*. Once you decide the freedom lifestyle is the only one you will ultimately accept, everything you do should be with that in mind. From your state of mind at your day job, to how you spend your free time, to your relationships. **Everything**.

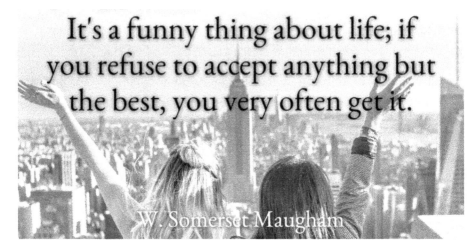

It's a funny thing about life; if you refuse to accept anything but the best, you very often get it.

W. Somerset Maugham

Can you imagine if your daily life suddenly became exhilarating, simply because you made a firm decision that the Ultimate Vida is the only life you desire?

There is something extremely powerful about making a firm decision that you refuse to accept any type of lifestyle that does not give you freedom. You'd be surprised how much momentum you can start building even if your daily life still "looks" the same for now on the surface. My days at work during the last few months of my job were a blur. I felt like a "secret agent" who would put on the suit and show up for one job while secretly plotting my escape into the life I really wanted. It was actually exhilarating.

Yes, you may still have to show up for your job tomorrow and next Monday, but if you suddenly know in your mind and heart that it's only a matter of time until you make the leap, just think about what you could start doing in the meantime:

- The big domino that will set everything into motion with that decision is related to the "B.O.S.S." (Be Of Supreme Service) Methodology I revealed a bit earlier. "Wait a minute, Jesse – what are you talking about? Who am I going to serve? And what am I going to serve them?" Glad you asked. ☺ I'll give you the exact roadmap to follow in a moment. Sneak preview: it involves the movie "Ghostbusters" (yes, really).

- Will you still live in the same place once you quit your job? Remember, you'll be calling your own shots and will have no geographic restrictions. Surroundings matter! Start researching your most desired areas and scoping out specific apartments, etc. Or would you prefer to be nomadic and just constantly travel, rather than having a home base? That will now be on the table, too. You can Airbnb various places around the world for days, weeks, or even months at a time. And by employing the ultra-powerful strategies of geo-arbitrage and seasonal arbitrage, you can completely bend this equation to your will!

- What kinds of environments will you want to work in? Again, surroundings matter! If you're going to stay local, start scoping out which coffee shops, restaurants, co-working spaces, parks, etc. you feel best in, as they just may soon become your virtual offices!

Waging War on Linear Thinking

We don't just start this research and "dreamwork" simply because it's exciting or inspiring. No! There's a much more important and powerful purpose at play. We do it to **kick linear thinking in the ass**. Yes, linear thinking is extremely dangerous, and can be seriously hazardous to your freedom lifestyle! What I mean by "linear thinking," is falling into the trap of "first this, then that." Or "once X happens, then I can do Y." No, no, no!

The ultimate example of linear thinking is to work for 40 years of your adult life building someone else's dream (your employer's) instead of your own, with the mere hope that one day in your 60s, you might be able to retire and enjoy your "golden years."

I know this is considered perfectly normal and reasonable by most of society. But is it just me, or is this actually sheer lunacy? Can I get an Amen?! I mean, why on Earth would one choose this path, when the option is open to us at any time to embark upon a life of absolute freedom starting right now, that is a beautiful and endless symphony of work, play, health, love, travel, and whatever else is important to you?

Action Steps
Check them off - literally, in ink!

Decide to be free

Choose one place you
would like to live for a month

Choose one place
you would like to 'work'

Step 2: You're Not Going to Get Out on Your Own

Why the "Ghostbusters Adjustment" is the Key to Unlocking Your Ultimate Vida

When I was growing up in the 80s, one of the coolest movies of the decade was *Ghostbusters*. It became quite a pop culture phenomenon, largely thanks to the line "Who you gonna call?"

Now, I may or may not have spent hours in front of the mirror trying to capture Ray Parker Jr's (one hit wonder?) swag, but that's a different story for a different time.

I do, however, have a true story for you that just happened and is far more relevant for you.

I was recently flown to Barcelona to teach the Ultimate Vida lifestyle at a small, private event, to a group of inspiring, courageous students who took massive action towards escaping the 9 to 5 and creating their own Ultimate Vida by flying in from around the world and immersing themselves in learning.

I had already completed my outline of what I was going to teach and felt good about it. So, I allowed myself to zone out and relax a bit on the plane. I opened up the movie directory on the in-flight entertainment system, clicked on a category called "Classics," saw *Ghostbusters* among the listings, and suddenly had an aha moment!

I feverishly paused the programming, ripped my headphones off, leapt out of my seat to grab my laptop from the overhead compartment, fired it up, and wrote down the "Ghostbusters Adjustment" which is THE key question and foundation for building your Ultimate Vida:

"Who You Gonna SERVE?"

That's it. Four words (Yes, Mom, "gonna" is a word) that will literally be your escape hatch from the 9 to 5 and your key to unlock your Ultimate Vida.

Before you think I've gone mad and am hallucinating myself into a giant marshmallow (bonus points if you're with me), lemme 'splain exactly how and why this question is your golden ticket.

There are two distinct levels for which answering the question "Who you gonna serve?" will set you free.

Level One: Exchanging *Value* for Money

Virtually everything in life is a trade of some kind.

In your 9 to 5, you are trading time for money. I've made this trade once in my adult life (if you count age 21-23 as being an "adult"), and it literally terrified me to the point of waking up in cold sweats as the next 40 years of my life flashed before me.

The danger of trading time for money is that it outright guarantees that you'll never be free. Even if you rise to the very highest level in your 9 to 5, while your paycheck may be very large, you'll stop getting it the moment you stop showing up to build your employer's dream rather than your own.

The money part of this trade isn't the problem. Money, I'm good with. As far as I'm concerned, whoever said that "money is the root of all evil" is insane. Money rocks. Money alone does not and cannot create meaning, let alone make us happy. But it absolutely can – and in fact must – be a central tool in crafting our Ultimate Vida.

So that brings us back to time. Time is life's great equalizer. The wealthiest person on the planet has exactly the same number of hours and minutes in each day as you and I do. And we each get to decide how to allocate these precious hours and minutes.

I'm going to assume that you buy into the premise that trading time for money is not an optimal exchange. Because if you thought it was, you'd just keep doing what you're doing, and would not have picked up this book.

We now come back full circle to our "Ghostbusters adjustment" question: *Who you gonna serve?*

This level of exchanging value for money is fairly straightforward. But don't be fooled. Its power lies in its simplicity. By "exchanging value for money," we simply mean that you're going to exchange products, services, information, or experiences to a group of people who have a certain desire; in exchange for their money (which they'll line up to pay you if you treat 'em right).

But we're going to set this exchange up for you in a way that does **not** require you to trade time for money. We're going to create a system by which people can access your solutions 24/7/365, no matter what you're doing (Including sleeping. Yes, waking up to money in your inbox is real. *Very* real. And it **never** gets old).

Put another way, you're going to exchange a *result* for money. You're either going to help people achieve a particular result that they desire, or just provide it for them. And if you do? Believe me when I say they won't give a damn how much time you spend doing it, whether you do it manually or automate it, or where in the world you do it from.

Action Steps
Check them off - literally, in ink!

Think of someone you would be happy to serve

Write down the highest figure you've ever heard of someone paying for education

Write down how many hours a day you would choose to 'work' if you had the choice

Step 3: How to Find the Inner Strength to Escape

Level Two of "Who You Gonna Serve": What's Your Ikigai? (Make it Bigger Than You)

Japan has the longest life expectancy of any country – 90 for women and 84 for men. And Okinawa is the best of the best in this regard, with over five times as many centenarians (people who live to 100) as anywhere else in Japan.

One main reason Okinawans cite for their longevity is the concept of "Ikigai," which translates to "A reason for being." In other words, a purpose greater than oneself. This harkens back to the "why," but on an even broader and deeper scale. What do you want to build or create? What do you want your life to stand for? What kind of ripple effect do you want to create, and what kind of legacy do you want to leave? These questions are at the very heart of our guiding question; "Who you gonna serve?"

Religion, faith and spirituality are way beyond the scope of this book and I'm not going to go there, but…

Have you ever noticed that when we have a purpose that's higher or greater than just ourselves and our own personal needs, we tend to operate at a higher level, and feel more energized and focused?

This rings truer than ever when it comes to sculpting our Ultimate Vida.

There are two main forms that "Making it bigger than you" can take.

The first is your immediate inner circle. Your family and/or your loved ones. If you have a partner and/or family whom you share the journey with; people you would do anything for, they will most certainly be a driving force as you re-script your life. Make sure to keep them front and center at all times, but especially in those moments when you're "not feeling it," for they will be your inspiration and guiding light.

If you don't yet have an inner circle – or even if you do – the second form of "Making it bigger than you" applies on a much grander scale:

What impact do you want to leave on the world? How do you want to touch the lives of people beyond your inner circle? What do you hope people say about you when you're no longer here? What will your life stand for?

A Deeply Personal Example of Ikigai in Action

I have written this book while my dad's been battling significant health issues. He's had several surgeries, and also has an ongoing condition, and we still don't know how things will play out.

During that time, my personal Ultimate Vida and what it means to me have changed quite a bit. The core concept of Ultimate Vida is freedom. Always has been, always will be. But freedom is a highly charged, sacredly intimate, and deeply personal word. My first up front target for freedom was leaving my day job. And I managed to do so by becoming a "secret agent" and a pioneer in the world of online business.

My next goal was financial freedom. Money, money, money. Not because I wanted to buy things; to this day I don't care much what kind of car I drive or watch I wear. But somehow without even giving it too much thought, I had this instinct that financial freedom was the Holy Grail. So I became insanely driven. First to replace my income. Then to double it, triple it and so on. Enough was never "enough."

After too much time and too much stubbornness, I finally realized that more money wasn't going to make anything better.

So my next obsession became world travel. As I shared with you, I've always been fascinated with world exploration since I was a little boy. But the irony is that after I quit my job, I was working so hard and so much that the trips were few and far between. I hadn't quite figured out the whole "digital nomad" thing yet, even though I'd gotten brief tastes of it.

So then with the same near-obsessive drive I used to make money, this time I channeled it towards traveling the world. I told myself that come hell or high water I would figure out how to make money on the road. Plus, I had a reasonable cushion built up by this point, which no doubt alleviated the pressure.

Not surprisingly, it turned out that making money on the road was pretty much the same gig as making money at home. I mean, what does working at home consist of, anyway? A phone and laptop. And last time I checked, laptops could be taken anywhere and phones work anywhere – even back in the "early days" of the 2000s.

But hitting rock bottom? Boy did that change everything. And while I've started the healing process and made progress, I'm still a work in progress as I shared with you.

And my dad's situation?

Even more so.

As I write this chapter, we're preparing for his fourth surgery, which will be the most invasive one yet. And where will I be? Right by my parents' side. Whether his recovery is a month or a year.

Tears well up as I write this. Tears of fear and uncertainty and love and wanting my dad to be ok. But also tears of profound gratitude for having the ability to be there with and for my parents.

Almost no one has that kind of freedom – including many people who make plenty of money – and it breaks my heart. Ask yourself honestly, if something were to happen to a loved one, and you wanted to drop everything and be there for them, could you? If not, it's ok – that's what this book is for. And that's what the Ultimate Vida is all about.

Action Steps
Check them off - literally, in ink!

Write down the names of the people in your inner circle

Write down one possible purpose for your life

Write one sentence you would like your inner circle to tell people after your death

Step 4: Putting the Team Together

What's going on here?
You've done some internal preparation - now it's time to learn how to build the team that will set you free

04

STEP 1 ⊙ STEP 2 ⊙ STEP 3 ⊙ STEP 4 ⊙ STEP 5 ⊙ STEP 6

STEP 7 ⊙ STEP 8 ⊙ STEP 9 ⊙ STEP 10 ⊙ STEP 11 ⊙ STEP 12 ⊙ STEP 13

Ghostbusters Adjustment – The Answer

OK, so you've bought into "Who you gonna serve" being the ultimate question for your Ultimate Vida. Cool beans! Now how the heck are we gonna answer it?

Glad you asked ☺

Let's Take an Uber to Africa…

I was recently in Los Angeles and called an Uber. When the driver arrived (his name was Michael), he greeted me politely, but it was clear that English was not his first language. I asked Michael where he was from, and he said Uganda. I queried Michael, "Do you like it better here or in Uganda?" His answer was swift and decisive. "I like it better there," he said. "In Africa, we do things in tribes. We all help each other. Here it feels like people are only concerned about themselves and their immediate families."

He didn't give his opinion in a bitter or angry way, and also acknowledged America as the "Land of Opportunity." But he was very clear about how central to life the tribal element is in Africa, and how much it's lacking here.

My Ride with Michael Stayed in My Head Like a Song on Repeat

After Michael dropped me off, I wished him well, said goodbye and gave him a generous tip. But our conversation wouldn't leave me alone. So I let it have its place at the table, and asked myself to dig deeper as to why that was. And two words made their way to the surface and persistently thumped away in my mind: **connection and belonging**.

Our Primal Craving for <u>Connection</u>

It's certainly not revolutionary to say that we as people have a deep longing for connection. But now more than ever, I think we'd be well-served to acknowledge this desire, and not suppress it. And more to the point, do something about it. In a fascinating paradox, I feel like social media simultaneously deserves significant blame and credit here.

It's all too easy to point the finger at social media for the breakdown in human connection. But I can say without a doubt that social media is directly responsible for some of my most cherished connections — connections that have blossomed into deeply meaningful real-life friendships and/or business relationships.

However, on the not so healthy side of the social media fence, it can be dangerously seductive. Hours and hours of scrolling through news feed updates that do nothing to enhance your life can roll by in a heartbeat. We can also have unhealthy levels of attachment to "vanity metrics" such as likes, shares and comments that have absolutely no relation to our worth or value. But the most harmful element of all in my view is when we mistake connecting online for connecting in the real world. Absolutely nothing – and yes, that includes video chat – will ever replace the energy of being face to face and sharing physical space with other human beings; whether your closest friends or someone you're meeting for the very first time.

Our Subconscious Desire for <u>Belonging</u>

Almost no one will consciously or rationally say that they crave belonging. And yet we all do. Craving connection is fairly straightforward. The desire for belonging, however, is more subtle but every bit as powerful. If we just seek connection with no rhyme or reason, it can turn into a drug of sorts — feeling great when it happens, but later leaving us wondering what we're doing or what the real purpose is. It can make us feel like we're ping-ponging from one connection to another, but with no unifying thread.

Hence, belonging. But let's make an important distinction. When it comes to your family and close friends, connection is more than enough in and of itself. Here, you don't need to "belong" to anything, because the connection itself between you and the other person is whole and complete.

Tribal Belonging

But there's another form of connection we crave. To Michael the Uber driver's point, we also crave the "tribal" element. Feeling like we're a part of something bigger than ourselves. Feeling like we're part of a group bound by common goals, dreams, desires, fears, frustrations and insecurities. Feeling like we're not alone on the journey, and that we've got brothers and sisters in arms. Man, I'm getting fired up even as I write this! The word for this is **belonging**. Feeling like you've "found your people" and that you're walking with them side by side in your quest for whatever you're trying to achieve.

So how do we take connection and belonging to a tangible level? How do we relate it to the tribal concept that Michael from Uganda, and so many others, cherish? Most of all, how does it tie into your Ultimate Vida journey, and how does it set you free?

Glad you asked. ☺ I believe it takes three levels...

Level One: Connect With a Mentor

Find someone who's walked the path you seek to walk, and who's willing, able and qualified to guide you along the way. I can tell you point blank that if you select me as your humble guide and mentor, it will be the honor of my lifetime, as I am very clear that my "Ikigai" is to set people around the world free and allow them to be their best and highest self. I also want to reiterate that I am not some vague or mystical figure. On the contrary, I hope that you and I get to share a cup of coffee or glass of wine somewhere along the way. And I hope I can learn from you, too. I may be the guide and mentor when it comes to Ultimate Vida, but I am very much a student when it comes to life. ☺

Level Two: Connect With a Tribe of Like-Minded People

You want to be "in the foxhole" with people in similar life situations with whom you share common goals, dreams, desires and insecurities. This takes the form of others who are reading this book, and the Ultimate Vida online community that you'll be able to join. But the UV community won't end online. There will be many opportunities to connect in person with your fellow UV freedom seekers.

Level Three: Start and Lead a Tribe of Your Own!

But the third and most powerful level? That will not only be deeply meaningful for you, but also has the power to set you free?

Start and lead a tribe of your own!

If the thought of this scares or intimidates you, don't worry! That's a good thing. Big and meaningful goals *should* scare you a bit. But doesn't it also excite you? The great thing is that by embracing level one (having a guide/ mentor) and level two (being part of the UV tribe) of connection and belonging, you'll have a road map for how to make this happen. And you'll be able to share the journey with me and other extraordinary, like-minded people. And before you know it, you may just give birth to a living, breathing tribe of your own. A tribe who can set you free financially, and more importantly, achieve amazing things and be a beautiful part of your life's work.

Your Tribe Are Your Brothers and Sisters

Let's put a bow on this tribal concept with some real talk.

You might be thinking, "What's with all this mushy talk? Brothers and sisters? They're not my family. I have a real family."

I hear you. And I'm not suggesting your tribe is going to show up at your next family gathering. (Although I spent last Christmas with a very dear friend of mine who has become like a brother to me, and his family. In another country, no less. And do you know where we met? In an online tribe just like the one I'm suggesting you build).

So, do you have to treat them like family to succeed? I don't know. Probably not. I suppose you could fake it, and you'd probably still succeed. But why would you? What do you actually lose by treating your tribe like family? By making an iron-clad pledge to them and to yourself to always have their backs? Absolutely nothing. You have nothing to lose, and everything to gain.

When you operate with this amount of love...this amount of integrity...this amount of heart space? It changes **everything**. It brings so much more soul and spark to your business and to your life.

And if you want to know my honest take on it? Your tribe IS your family. Just as YOU are MY family. Not by blood, of course. But we're mirrors of each other! I have walked the exact path you're walking. Sure, some of the details and cast of characters are different. But I definitely know some of your most intimate hopes, dreams, fears, desires, questions and insecurities. I am so deeply passionate about you freeing yourself from the current constructs of your life and being able to create your own Ultimate Vida in all its glory. So, you better damn well believe I'm going to treat you like family.

And I feel very confident in saying that I will have the good fortune of meeting many of you reading this book in person one day over a glass of wine or a cup of coffee – which, along with water, are my three main beverages of choice, in case you were wondering. And I can only hope that you might choose to pay it forward and make it your business to build and hear and feel the heartbeat of your own tribe, and genuinely enrich their lives.

Now, if there's one central promise you hear me making throughout this book, it's that the principles and framework I show you will be timeless, right? Well, it doesn't get more timeless than building a tribe. Tribes have been around practically since the beginning of time. Tribes were around even before language. Tribes existed thousands of years ago, and they'll continue to exist thousands of years from now. Sure, the mechanisms, media and mediums will change. But that's not really the central point. It helps to stay current, of course, and that's why I've got the constantly updated list of resources available for you at www.UltimateVida.com/toolbox. But if you master the concepts between the two covers of this book, you'll be good to go no matter what the technology or business trend du jour. That's a powerful position to be in, wouldn't you say?

Unmasking Your Tribe

Let's drill down a bit further as to what this concept of "tribe" actually looks like. Your "tribe" can have two different levels. The first is mandatory, the second optional — but very helpful if you can make it happen.

Level One: Lovin' on Your Tribe

The first level is the relationship between you and your tribe. But while the concept of tribe implies community and group, this first level is actually all about a series of one-to-one relationships. Namely, the personal relationship between you and each member of your tribe.

In the next step, I'm going to start showing you how to develop a matrix-level, uber knowledge of your audience and who they are as people — the deep understanding that will make you a profoundly powerful tribal leader.

But even before that, I can show you an incredibly straightforward way to bring your tribe to life.

You may be surprised to learn that one of my core business philosophies is:

"The ultimate competitive advantage is LOVE."

Now, before you go thinking how "woo woo" or "new agey" this is, let me assure you that I am extremely analytical when it comes to business, and am as conscious of the bottom line as anyone. So as counter-intuitive as this philosophy may seem, it's actually extremely pragmatic.

What does this philosophy mean in the real world of business, then? What type of "love," exactly, am I talking about?

Quite simply, I mean **treat the people in your market or audience (your tribe) like family**.

Never forget that behind the "audience size of 1,314,962" or the "affinity score of 728%" (these terms will soon make a lot more sense) exists a group of human beings who share common hopes, dreams, fears, goals and desires.

You want to communicate with each of them on a very personal, intimate level. You want to elicit nods and smiles and laughs, and sometimes even *tears*, when you communicate with them – whether in writing, video, phone or in person.

You want them to feel like you really "get them" – because you genuinely *do* get them.

And the way to do that is with *love*. When you're getting ready to communicate with your audience, forget the word "audience." Act as if you are communicating with only one person. Imagine you are speaking to him or her directly. Better yet, *imagine that he or she were your mother, brother, sister or best friend*.

What tone would you take? What kind of words would you use? What would be your core message?

It's not about "marketing" or "business." It's simply about being real and helping these people solve their problems and move in the direction they want to go. You do this by opening the door through love and empathy, and then once it's open, providing practical solutions that they are <u>already seeking</u>.

Trust me when I say that this is the key to everything. This is the great equalizer.

In fact, let me double down on that.

You can be average at marketing, average at business, average at management, average at accounting, average at just about every specific skill and still create your own Ultimate Vida so magical that you'll have to pinch yourself to remind you that it's real – if you just do one thing: Deeply understand your audience, treat 'em like family, and give 'em what they want. Over and over and over again.

Level Two: Your Tribe Takes on a Life of its Own

The second level of this "tribal vibe" you want to build involves connecting the people you're reaching not only with you, but with each other. Whether that be online, in person, or both. That's where you can really build something that starts to take on a life of its own. That can be not only a business, but a movement or revolution. By making it much bigger than yourself, and "getting out of the way" in a sense, you actually bind them to you on a far deeper and longer-lasting level. Plus, it can get exhausting being the only voice that these people are waiting to hear. ☺

Now, getting people to communicate with each other on YOUR platform isn't always the easiest thing in the world. When you reach that point, the Ultimate Vida community will be a great place for you to get detailed, practical action plans. But as a brief overview, you'll be off to a great start if you:

- Have VERY clear guidelines that your community will NOT accept ANY unkind or negative communication. (Nothing will kill it off faster than letting people behave as if they're on Twitter.)

- Commit to answering EVERY SINGLE COMMENT for the first six months, which is a serious effort on your part, but it models how to be helpful, and will trigger copycat behavior.

- Do something extra to help one person each month, as a show of gratitude for their contribution to the forum —hop on a call with them, give them a bit of your expertise, and state openly in your community that you were grateful for something specific and positive that they contributed.

Those three core steps will point your community in the direction of being a place where people feel safe and supported, and grateful to you —which will lead to them contributing more and more over time, and eventually taking ownership of the nature of the community. They'll take pride in being a kind and friendly and supportive group of people.

Action Steps
Check them off - literally, in ink!

Write down the name of your ideal mentor

Claim the number of people you would like to help escape

Write down a name for your tribe

Step 5: Which Way Should This Tunnel Go?

"OK, Jesse, that's all great. But how the heck do I figure out what kind of tribe to start? Who will be in it? And what will be the topic?"

Glad you asked. ☺

There are two answers to this question. Level one is the general answer, which applies to all of us (I'll just give to you — you're welcome ☺). The general answer to our question "Who you gonna serve?" is as follows:

A group of people who are passionate about a certain topic and are hungry for solutions to their challenges related to this topic.

Business terms you'll sometimes hear used for these groups of people are "market" or "niche."

In plain English? Find people who are starving and feed 'em!

"But where and how do I identify these groups of people, Jesse? And once I do, how do I evaluate the business potential and figure out if I can make money?"

Here's where we get into the exciting part. The level two part, which becomes your specific answer, and eventually your specific tribe! This is the part that'll be unique to you and ultimately set you free! The foundation for **your** Ultimate Vida! Huge and exciting stuff! Don't worry, I'll help you uncover it in just a few seconds...

How to Find Your People & Build Your Tribe

Fundamentally, there are two ways you can find these groups of people, serve them, and make money to fund your freedom lifestyle: Passion-based and non-passion-based.

I'm sure you've heard clichés such as:

- "Do what you love and the money will follow"
- "If you do what you love, you'll never work another day in your life"

And you know what? Clichés are clichés for a reason. There's a lot of truth in them.

But if I told you it was a requirement to be passionate about the way you make money, I'd be lying. I've had online businesses in topics ranging from classic cars to golf to babies to document conversion to knitting (yes, knitting!). What do these five topics have in common? I know absolutely nothing about them!

So yes, it can be done. But when I compare those businesses to what I get to do now, which is to help you create and live your Ultimate Vida?! Well, there really isn't even any comparison. I feel like the luckiest guy in the world to be able to call this "work."

Settling the "Great Passion Debate"

My take on the "passion debate" goes something like this. If you are passionate about business and marketing itself, it almost doesn't matter what your product or service is (as long as there's a demand for it – we'll get into that in a minute!). But if you're not? I'd strongly recommend going down a path you're passionate about.

I'm not going to get on my soapbox and tell you that you have to "do something that fulfills you" to be happy. I'm no one to judge what makes you happy. Besides, being your own boss, making money on your own terms, and taking back your life may be more than enough to make you happy!

Here's my final word on the "passion debate" (I promise!). And it's a key point that I haven't even seen the "gurus" talk about. You can totally make money in areas you're not passionate about. We've already established that. But – and it's a big but (not a big butt – no pun intended!) – if you're going down this route, your mindset, motivation and mental game better be *extremely* strong. Because I guarantee you, there are going to be days and moments when you do NOT feel like doing certain things that will advance your Ultimate Vida.

But if your money-making vehicle is tied to something you're passionate about? *It changes the game completely.*

For example, I can honestly say that I never get bored or tired even for a moment about sharing and teaching the Ultimate Vida. It lights me up and inspires me at such a deep, core level that it gives me the chills every time I think about it.

So, while it's not required... trust me when I say that if we can get to what gives *you* the chills?

It'll dramatically stack the odds in your favor. It'll make it infinitely easier to gather steam and build momentum. It'll make you feel like you're riding downhill and catching the wave, rather than every day being a struggle and grind.

There's a powerful diagram that has become one of my "go to" frameworks over the years for developing new business ideas:

FINDING YOUR CRAFT/STYLE

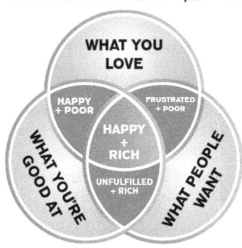

As you can see, there are three categories:

- What you're good at
- What you love to do
- What people want (and will pay you for)

And the "sweet spot" is where all three intersect! Here's the exact three-step process on how to find it. You'll need three sheets of paper, and a pen. That's it. Ready? Go!

Step One: Make a List of Everything You're Good At

Take your first sheet of paper and start answering the following questions in free-flow:

- What comes easily to you?
- What are some things people come to you for help with?
- What do you tend to do better than most people? You don't have to be the best in the world at it – just do it at a higher level than most.

List everything you can think of here, whether it's something you like to do or not. Literally any skill in life that you're good at. Doesn't matter if it's a work skill or life skill, professional or personal. No filtering, no editing, and don't worry how tiny or insignificant a certain skill might seem. List it anyway!

Step Two: Make a List of Everything You're Passionate About

- Put your first sheet of paper away or turn it over, take out your second sheet, and start answering the following questions:
- What magazines do you subscribe to?
- What blogs do you read?
- What are your most frequently visited sites when you surf the web?
- What books is Amazon suggesting for you?
- What are the topics of any clubs or meetup groups that you're a part of?
- What are the topics of any Facebook groups or other online groups you're a part of?
- What are your favorite activities to pursue when you're not working?
- What do you do when you lose track of time? This one is by far my

favorite. It takes a bit more thought, but is so incredibly revealing. You know that feeling of being "in the zone," where everything just flows and hours pass by in what feels like minutes? That's what we're looking for here. What do you find yourself doing when this happens? Write it down, bold it, and highlight it!

Step Three: How to Make Sure the Money Will Follow Your Passions!

Pull out your lists from step 1 and step 2, and place them side by side. In this step, you don't have to answer any questions, and you only have one goal: to identify answers & topics that appear on both your first and second sheets! Every time you identify one, highlight it or put a check mark next to it so that it stands out and you'll be able to come back to it.

Once you've finished going through both lists and identifying the entries that appear on both, simply copy them onto your third sheet of paper. Don't worry if you have one item or 50. Just put 'em on that final sheet.

Now you've got a list of thing(s) that you're both good at, and passionate about! But there's one more crucial step, and it's where most people drop the ball and waste agonizing amounts of time and money spinning their wheels in futility. But you're not going to do that. **You're not going to commit the cardinal sin** of falling in love with an idea or topic without first verifying if people are actually spending money in that market.

(Note: do NOT worry at this point about "what you're going to sell." That comes later, and for that matter, there are ways to make money from a market without selling anything at all. Right now, our only objective is to find out if money is changing hands in some form in any of the categories that you listed on your third sheet of paper, which goes back to that "sweet spot" on our trusty diagram!)

Picking Your Winner

By now, you should have a small handful of ideas that you are:

- Good at; and
- Love doing!

Now the key is find out which of them you can also make money from! This is the "Happy and Rich" sweet spot of the Venn diagram I shared with you a moment ago!

But before we do? Here are a few questions to NOT ask yourself yet (most people start with these questions and shoot themselves in the foot):

- What will I sell?
- Will I offer products or services?
- Will they be my own products & services, or affiliate offers?
- Will I also do coaching or develop courses?
- Do I need to start a Facebook group or a YouTube channel?
- What kind of software or technical tools will I need?
- Do I have to put on events?

I can already feel your tension rising, as these thoughts and questions race through your mind. And I've got one key word for you that'll hopefully put your mind at ease:

RELAX ☺

I have seen each and every one of the models above work very well. I have also made money from markets where I sell absolutely nothing at all (yes, it's possible).

This journey is about creating *your* Ultimate Vida. Not mine or anyone else's. It's about playing to your strengths and desires, and setting up a structure where you can make money doing something you love, while having the freedom and mental space to make the impact you desire! Does it really get any better than that? I literally just got the chills as I wrote that for you! Soak it in, smile, and get ready. Here we go...

Time to Slip On Your Pair of Ultimate Vida 3D Glasses

We are about to do some seriously next-level spy work. Matrix-level market research that'll have you playing chess while others play checkers – always a move or two ahead. Even many of the most advanced entrepreneurs and marketers in the world are not aware of a great deal of the tools and tactics I'm about to show you. And of those who are aware, only a precious few are actually applying them. So, you're about to gain a *major* unfair advantage!

First, though, I want to double down on the promise I made to you in the intro of this book. Remember I said that everything I show you will be timeless, not trendy and will work as well in five or 10 years as it does now?

I stand by that 100%, and here are two very important points:

1. Each of the tools I'm about to show you have been around for well over a decade, and I don't see them going anywhere.

2. But if any of them do go away? Or better yet, are replaced by something even more powerful or effective? I've created a special "toolbox" page for you at www.UltimateVida.com/toolbox that I'll always keep up to date. The tools may change, but the concepts are timeless!

With that point in mind, let's jump in!

Conversations and Toll Booths?

Entering the Conversation Inside Their Heads

People are constantly having conversations – both with others, and inside their own heads. The key to being of service (and making money) in any market is to enter the conversation in their minds.

Note: most marketers get this completely wrong. They try to change the conversation people are having, rather than enter the one that's already going on. This is like trying to swim against the current instead of floating with it.

Making money from any market ultimately comes down to understanding the people in that market on a very intimate level.

You are going to become their best friend, their trusted advisor, their soulmate, their confidant, without them even knowing it. You're going to understand their deepest pains, fears, challenges, dreams, hopes and desires. On some levels, you're going to know them even better than they know themselves.

Then, once you've entered that conversation? You're going to set up a virtual toll booth that is located along the path that they're already going, and collect a small fee (which they'll gladly fork over!) as they pass by.

If any of this sounds sneaky or nefarious? Fear not, you're going to be a superhero and use this information only for their highest good, by offering them solutions that genuinely improve their lives!

Now, before I hand you your pair of Ultimate Vida 3D Glasses and we jump into some Matrix-level research, I need to say one more thing. It may not be popular or politically correct, but it's the truth and it needs to be said.

All people Inside Your Market are *NOT* Created Equal

I'm not talking about intrinsic value here, or saying that anyone is a more worthy person than anyone else. What I'm saying is that when it comes to being of service – and making money – you need to look at a very specific subset of your market. This subset is the "group within your group" that will show you how to monetize (make money from) this market.

How do I know this? Well, I've been marketing online since 1998, and during that time I've had many different businesses in dozens of different markets. One of the key metrics we measure is called sales conversion rate. Which simply means the percentage of people who see your stuff online that actually spend money on your solutions. I can tell you that a conversion rate over 10% is almost unheard of. Usually I shoot for 3-5%, but depending on the business model, even 1% can be very profitable. Heck, I had a client who built a multi-million dollar business and made the Inc. 500 list with a 0.5% conversion rate!

Why does this matter to you? Well... when we talk about "entering the conversation inside their mind," the conversations we really want to locate and listen to are the ones taking place among a very small subset of your audience. Not the casual fans, but the *rabid* ones. People who are unreasonably interested in your topic. People who are **irrationally passionate**. Hungry to the point of starving. People who are not just researching a casual interest or talking for the sake of talking, but who are ready to take action to find a solution to their problems. People who are *obsessed*. Now, let's go and find 'em!

3D Glasses Tool #1: Forums

You know what's amazing? On the Internet, these "conversations inside their heads" get downloaded into written form. They literally play out constantly, in real time, before your very eyes, and are available to you 24/7! Pretty cool, huh?

Long before Facebook, Instagram & Twitter – heck, even before Google – the Internet was built on forums. Back then, they were called message boards. And they're still alive and well, and are one of your best sources to learn what's really going on inside the minds of your people. If you're thinking forums are "old school?" A good friend of mine recently sold his online forum for a 7-figure sum! Forums will always have their place, and offer a level of depth and focus that social media cannot match.

Not all topics have forums online, but many do. To find out if yours does, all you have to do is fire up Google and type in your topic plus "forums" or "message boards." So, if your topic is meditation, for example, your search would look like "meditation forums" or "meditation message boards."

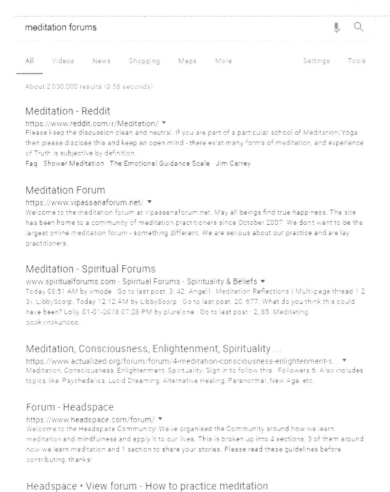

Now, this graphic only shows the top six listings, simply because otherwise it would take up the entire page or be too small to read. But you can easily replicate the search yourself in Google.

So, let's talk about the first few things I'd do and be looking for when I see the search results for forums on any market I'm considering entering. Note that the key word here is **market**, which is simply the "business term" for these groups of people you want to serve.

We are NOT looking to validate or invalidate a specific product or service idea at this stage (in fact, it's probably premature to even *have one*). What we're doing at this stage is evaluating the business potential of the **market as a whole**.

First, I'd scroll through the first few pages of listings to take the general pulse of what the forum landscape looks like for this topic. I typically look at the first three to five pages of listings, which are 30-50 listings total (10 on each page). I find that's a good sweet spot for getting an accurate read of what's going on without getting too crazy.

If there are NOT any forums on your topic, it's not a total deal breaker, but I'd definitely consider it a red flag. There are two reasons why it's not a total deal breaker:

First, because there are several research tools that I use (the rest of which I'll reveal in the coming pages) to validate or invalidate a market, and forums are only one of them.

And second, while forums are still alive and well, and honestly I don't see them going anywhere, I have seen a slight decrease in forum activity on a macro level as other forms of community such as Facebook groups have risen in popularity.

That said, forums are still gold and offer a level of focus, singularity and lack of distraction that no social media platform will ever come close to matching.

OK, now let's say that the search results do show a handful of forums around a topic. So far, so good! Looks promising at first glance. So next, we'd want to start clicking into these forums to check them out. Continuing with our search results above, I'd probably skip the first Reddit listing (Reddit is a whole other beast – there are some golden nuggets in there, but they can be hidden among lots of "interesting" stuff). So in this case, I'd start with listing #2, which has the heading "Meditation Forum" and we can see by the URL happens to relate to Vipassana meditation.

Note: I happen to be into meditation and know that Vipassana is a central form of meditation and is very relevant. However, if I didn't know that, I'd keep scrolling until I see more general looking forums, and here's what

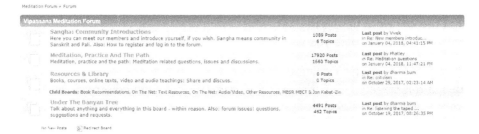

we'd get (further note: sometimes you'll get taken to the site's home page rather than the forum page. If this happens, simply click on the link that says "forum," "message board," or something similar):

The results above are very typical of a "forum home page." A few broad topics are listed, which you can click on to open up and view the content and sub-topics. There are three main things I'm looking for here:

1. Do the broad topics seem relevant?

2. Is this an active and thriving forum with lots of posts?

3. What is the recency of the latest posts (i.e. is the forum active NOW)?

In this case, the answer to question #1 — do the broad topics seem relevant? – is yes, in my view – particularly the second category: Meditation, Practice, And The Path (note that this category also has the highest number of topics and posts by a wide margin).

The answer to #2 — is this an active and thriving forum with lots of posts? — is also a clear yes in my view. The most active category has 1,660 topics and 17,920 posts! That is seriously thriving without a doubt. I'm typically looking for activity in the hundreds at a minimum. If it's over 1,000, even better. So, to see these numbers is very encouraging.

You'll have to use your judgment here to some extent, though. If you're looking at a fairly broad topic like meditation, you'll want to see larger numbers. However, if it's a tighter niche you're considering, there can sometimes be active forums with just a few hundred posts.

Note: in most cases, the smaller the niche, the better, because you're able to talk to the people in the niche in a far more personal manner and really tap into their emotions. So, in this case, if I were to enter the meditation market, I would NOT just take a broad, sweeping angle such as "how to meditate" as

I'd almost be guaranteeing that I'd fail. Instead, I'd focus on a certain form or technique of meditation (such as Vipassana!) or target certain sub-segments of the population (i.e. meditation for entrepreneurs, meditation for moms, etc).

The answer to question #3 — what is the recency of the latest posts (i.e. is the forum active NOW?) — is **as strong a yes as you can possibly get**. I wrote this chapter of the book on January 4, 2018, so it is very encouraging to see that the latest posts in this forum are from the same day! Doesn't get much fresher than that.

Now let's dig deeper by clicking on the most active segment of this forum (Meditation, Practice, And The Path), and see what we find and how to analyze the results...

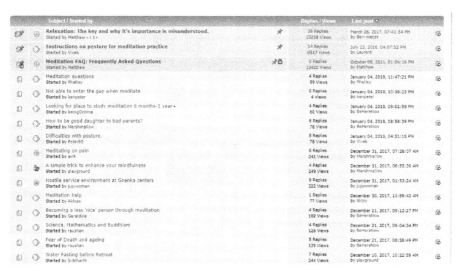

The three shaded threads at the top are known as "sticky" threads, meaning they are timeless threads that will always appear at the top, above the ongoing content. These often contain FAQs, rules & instructions of the forum, etc.

Note that the default sort here is the "last post" column, which shows the most recent posts first. This is very important, because when considering entering any market, you want to know what topics are current and trendy.

However, it's even more important to know which are the most popular or "hottest" topics in your market, as when there are many people talking about a topic instead of just a few, it's a sign that there's a serious pressing

Subject / Started by	Replies / Views	Last post
Relaxation: The key and why it's importance is misunderstood. Started by Matthew «1 2»	39 Replies 20,258 Views	March 26, 2017, 07:41:54 PM by Ben-meijer
Meditation FAQ: Frequently Asked Questions. Started by Matthew	0 Replies 13422 Views	October 08, 2011, 01:06:16 PM by Matthew
Instructions on posture for meditation practice. Started by Vivek	14 Replies 8817 Views	July 23, 2016, 04:07:52 PM by Laurent
TERRIBLE and TRAUMATIC experience at Goenka retreat. Started by DJ Shaka «1 2 3 4 ... 6»	132 Replies 105446 Views	April 05, 2017, 05:59:37 PM by Manohar Shrestha
Meditation is causing insomnia for me - why? Started by DANE01 «1 2 3 4»	78 Replies 42216 Views	April 18, 2011, 02:31:08 AM by Andrew
Stream Entry on a Goenka 10 Day Course? Started by seekongñana «1 2 3 4 5»	101 Replies 42197 Views	January 31, 2011, 11:01:16 PM by Lokuttara
Zazen Vs Vipassana. Started by faltu «1 2»	42 Replies 42113 Views	December 03, 2010, 11:14:24 AM by Matthew
Trembling and Shaking whilst Meditating. Started by Nicki	18 Replies 35599 Views	June 11, 2013, 05:48:04 PM by focusing
How has meditation changed your life? Started by Copey «1 2 3»	74 Replies 31198 Views	October 22, 2012, 12:50:56 PM by Sylvia1982
Meditation and alcohol. Started by hestorsisten	11 Replies 26300 Views	May 15, 2013, 09:36:30 AM by alpha82
meditation and sexual drive. Started by RusskiPower «1 2 3»	52 Replies 25847 Views	September 19, 2013, 01:04:02 AM by DarkNightOfNoSoul
What is the best practice? Started by VinceField «1 2 3 4 ... 5»	125 Replies 23703 Views	September 02, 2014, 03:40:12 PM by Matthew
Struggling in calm abiding meditation. Started by ramelec «1 2 3 4»	90 Replies 22349 Views	March 17, 2011, 09:51:45 AM by Matthew
Some interesting points by Ajahn Amaro. Started by Crystal Palace «1 2 3 4»	83 Replies 21962 Views	June 25, 2011, 10:45:03 PM by Morning Dew
Meditation Journal. Started by alpha_wolf «1 2 3 4 5»	113 Replies 21736 Views	May 15, 2016, 09:17:38 PM by Matthew
Ex Goenka practisioners Survivors Group. Started by shendy «1 2 3»	61 Replies 21471 Views	October 20, 2010, 02:12:55 PM by Lokuttara

need that you can find a solution for. So, what I'd do here is re-sort by the middle column (replies/views), and here's what we'd get (note: you want to make sure that you're sorting from most activity to least, so sometimes you might have to click the column twice to make sure the sort is going in the right order:

These results are very interesting, and a perfect case study to illustrate how to evaluate a market and its hot buttons! The two key things we're looking for here are views and replies. Views tell us which posts grab people's attention, while replies take it a step further and call out the more passionate members of the audience who not only want to read, but choose to engage and make their voice heard. These are the people we want to pay particularly close attention to.

You'll notice that the top result when we sort by views is titled "Terrible and traumatic experience at Goenka resort." Now at first glance, I would think to myself that this is not particularly relevant information, as it just refers to a negative experience at a certain resort. Nevertheless, it's notable that it's the most viewed thread in this topic!

But as I scroll down the top threads by views, I see (to my surprise) that there are three separate threads on that first page about this particular resort! So, while it's still likely an outlier, it's now risen to the level where I'd open up a new tab and Google it.

When I do this, I discover one Satya Narayan Goenka, an Indian teacher of meditation who died fairly recently, in 2013. I also discover that he's considered a key figure in the evolution of Vipassana meditation, and that there are meditation centers in his name not just in India, but around the world.

What I'd do at this point is make a mental note of Goenka and a few literal notes in my research file (you'll want to have a Word doc or Notepad file open while you do this exercise). And I would now continue scanning down the listings, looking for the next most popular topic after Goenka.

Boom! The very next listing talks about meditation causing insomnia. A few listings down is a thread about meditation and alcohol, followed by another about meditation and sexual drive.

These are threads that I would pay seriously close attention to. Why? Because now we're getting into pain points and emotionally distressing situations. Meaning we're likely entering **urgency territory**.

With urgency comes motivation to take action. And issues like sleep, drinking and sex are right up there in terms of universally important and emotional issues! So, if we can figure out a way to create solutions involving meditation to improve people's sleep or sex life, or reduce their drinking, these solutions would likely be very much in demand.

Again, we're not looking to come up with actual product or service ideas quite yet at this stage – we're just investigating to uncover what the key problems, challenges and pain points are in this space, and what types of potential solutions would be welcomed.

As we open up the first thread about meditation and insomnia, we see the following question posed in 2011 by an individual from Denmark:

Now, let's talk about the date for a moment. Your first thought may be "2011 is too old and no longer current." This is a perfectly valid thought to have. And in many markets – perhaps even the majority – that are based on trendiness and current events, that could be a deterrent. But in this case, I'd say it's not, for two reasons:

First, even though the original question was posed in 2011, the thread has been alive and well the entire time, and the most recent response was the exact day I did the search. This tells us that the topic is still very relevant and timely.

Second, meditation itself is about as evergreen of a market as I can think of. It's been around for thousands of years, and will be around for thousands more. I personally happen to love evergreen markets that I can do business in for many years or decades, and that are not impacted by trends, seasons, or current events.

I would then start scrolling through people's responses. There are three main things I'd be looking for:

First and most importantly, I'd be looking for multiple people basically giving the same or very similar answers. This would suggest to me that it's likely to be more accurate or credible. But even so, it wouldn't be sufficient on its own.

Which is why **secondly**, I'd be looking for answers that cite other resources (publications, articles, websites, videos, etc) to back up their opinion.

And **thirdly**, I usually add slightly more weight to answers that come from moderators or people associated with that particular forum, as chances are they have a degree of expertise with that topic.

I would then repeat this process for the threads about meditation/sex and meditation/alcohol, again using the criteria above, and again cataloguing my findings in my Word doc. Remember, the entire purpose of this exercise at this stage is to simply identify whether or not:

- there are gaps in the marketplace,
- these gaps feel like emotional hot buttons (and preferably timeless ones), and
- it appears that if solutions were to be provided, people would be interested in pursuing said solutions.

Again, we are NOT yet thinking about whether we're going to deliver products or services, ebooks, videos, membership sites, etc. That will come later. There are an almost infinite amount of ways to monetize a market by offering products and services in various formats; and there are also ways to make money from a market without having to deliver products or services at all!

What I would do next is go back to the Google listings for meditation forums and find a couple more forums and repeat the process above. That may seem too anal or detail oriented, but the way I look at it, is I want to stack the odds in my favor as much as possible of succeeding, and that does not usually mean basing my decision on one forum only.

Let's say for the sake of argument that I look through a couple more forums and things still look promising. At this point, my evaluation would be that the meditation market (and possibly Vipassana meditation) has passed the first test in my research.

Now we're going to kick things up a notch, and see if people are actually spending money in this market! And if so, what are they buying? A very important question, wouldn't you agree?

3D Glasses Tool #2: Udemy

It's amazing to me how Udemy just keeps flying under the radar, year after year. Most of the other 3D resources I recommend, people are familiar with or have at least heard of – they just don't know how to use them for maximum benefit. But Udemy? Not so much. So, here's the deal. Udemy is an online learning marketplace where courses in all kinds of topics are taught – and access to these courses is sold.

The key word here is **sold**. Because as I promised you, now we're going to kick things up a notch! It's one thing to see what people are "interested in," but it's quite another to see what they're willing to take out their wallet for! And that is the beauty of Udemy.

Note that Udemy does include some free courses. But the majority are paid, and you'll always be able to see within any given market, how many of the courses are paid vs. free (which is a valuable indicator in and of itself – we'll get to that in a moment).

And as with all my resources, my "timeless principles" promise to you will always stand. So, if at any time, a better resource than Udemy becomes available that achieves the same goal, I'll keep things updated for you at www.UltimateVida.com/toolbox.

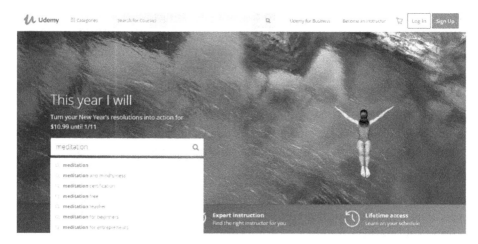

With that said, let's jump in! We're going to head over to Udemy.com and type in "meditation" in the main search box to take the general pulse of the marketplace and see if any courses are being offered...

OK, before I show you the results of our search, look what happened when I typed in "meditation." See all those suggestions that popped up? They are there for a reason. These are sub-topics within the broad category of meditation.

In fact, I even see my "meditation for entrepreneurs" idea in their suggestions – and I hadn't even consulted this list yet! At any rate, these "suggestions" that Udemy offers are super useful information! You'll definitely want to add them to your research file as you proceed.

OK, with that said, now let's look at our actual search results...

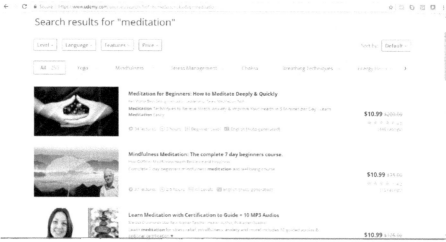

There is a LOT of valuable information to unpack here, so let's get right to it:

- The screenshot only captures the first three results, but the first thing to note is that there are no fewer than 259 results for meditation! (See box labeled "All" in upper left.) This means that there are 259 separate courses being sold in this online marketplace related in some way to meditation. I'd consider this a very good initial indicator.

- Next to the "All" button, notice that various sub-topics are listed, with a number next to them (Yoga, mindfulness, stress management, etc). These are the related or sub-topics to meditation that have the highest amounts of courses being sold. They appear in order. For example, yoga is first with 30 courses available). Makes sense, as yoga and meditation have obvious synergy. However, personally, my interest would be more piqued by "mindfulness," because it's more directly aligned with meditation, more in line with my personal interests, AND has almost as many courses being sold (29) as yoga so the market potential is equally potent.

- The "level" drop-down menu shows that there are both beginner and intermediate level courses being offered. This is encouraging, as it's far easier to make money in a market when you can reach people at various stages of the journey. It also opens the possibility down the road of having repeat customers who start at beginner level, and keep moving up to more advanced and/or customized solutions that you provide.

- The "language" drop-down menu shows that after English, Dutch and French are the next two popular languages for meditation courses! This can be very useful data as well, as it's easier than ever to get coursework translated and enter into other geo-markets.

- In the "price" drop-down menu, we discover that 238 of the 260 meditation courses are paid, and only 22 are free. That's 92%! Very encouraging.

Now let's turn our attention to the drop-down menu in the upper right, which allows us to sort the results by price, date, most reviewed, and highest rated — all in ascending or descending order.

I start by sorting the results by price, and find that the lowest-priced course is $10.99, and the highest is $200! That is quite a healthy range, and a positive sign for the reasons I mentioned above.

Now let's talk about the user reviews – because this is a **freaking goldmine**. There are a few ways we want to use this information:

- Start by sorting by "highest rated." The reason for this is because if you do end up eventually entering whatever market you're researching, you're probably going to want to model the most popular and successful offerings rather than the least. Right?!

- Click into the reviews of the highest-rated courses and start reading through them to identify trends and repeated words/themes that people liked. Note these in your research file, as you'll definitely want to include them if/when you enter the market. It's important to know whether people liked a product, but it's even more important to know *why*.

- Even the best-rated courses will have some negative reviews. These are important to study too, so that you can understand the shortcomings and what's missing. These are the gaps in the marketplace that you can potentially step in and fill (and be the hero!). Again, it's important to look for trends and *repeated* complaints, as opposed to just one person's opinion.

Next, you'll want to sort by the "Most reviewed" column. I can't stress how valuable this information is. In fact, let's take a look at the results, and get into why it's so valuable. ☺

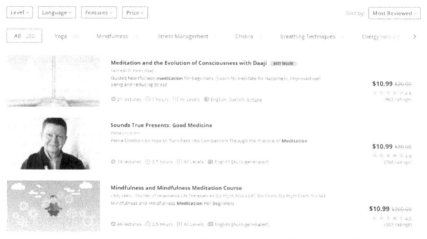

The screenshot only allowed for the first three results, but that's plenty to explain the concept. The key point to keep in mind here is that these are paid courses. So, for example, the fact that the most-reviewed course above has 902 reviews means that many more than 902 people bought the product! I usually find that around 20-30% of the people who buy a course leave a review. Meaning that this course has done over $30,000 on Udemy alone (and probably far, far more, as they're likely marketing elsewhere as well).

Do you realize how valuable it is to just have free and open access to see exactly which courses are selling in any given market, how many copies, and at what price? This is the kind of market research data that corporations traditionally have paid millions for! And it's just freely available. Pretty amazing.

Now, the final thing you'll want to do here is check the top-selling courses in whatever market you're researching, to see what their format is, and how they've broken down the content. When you do this, prepare to be **stunned** once again by the wealth of information you find. For example, here's what I found when I clicked into the top selling meditation course:

First, we see the course title, sub-head and key topics and bullet points:

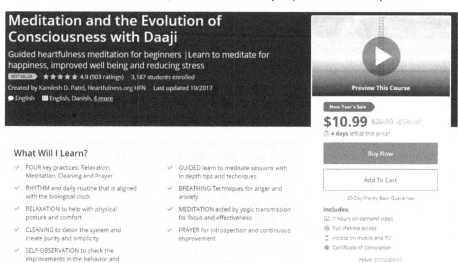

The best approach is to always model what's proven to work. And any course that is the top-selling offer in its category is most certainly proven to work! We never under any circumstances want to copy, but we do want to model. Everything from the headline, sub-head, bullet points, etc. We can offer our own twist or spin on things, but it behooves us to follow templates of what works.

Next, we have a course description followed by some testimonials:

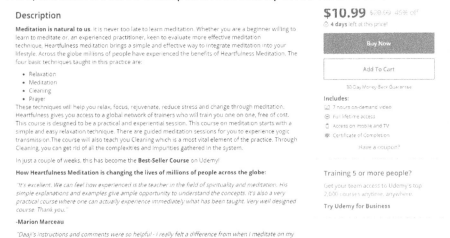

Again, we want to model what works! The point here is not to copy their Udemy listing. First of all, we never want to copy. Second, we may or may not even sell any work on Udemy. (I usually don't.) The underlying point is that these are the types of headlines, sub-heads, bullet points, and descriptions that the best-selling course in the marketplace is using. We can adapt these to our eventual websites, emails, social media content, webinars, or whatever format we eventually present our material in. Useful stuff! ☺

Finally, perhaps the most valuable data of all here – the course curriculum!

Before we get into the curriculum, notice at the top of the page, Udemy tells us exactly how many students have enrolled in this course – 3,187! So in this case, 903 out of 3,187 students left a review, but 3,187 bought at $10.99, for a total of $35,025.13 in sales! And that's from Udemy alone, which is likely a tiny fraction of their overall sales. Not too shabby.

OK, let's look at the curriculum. Again, an absolute goldmine of information. This tells us how the course is broken down, how many lectures (21), how much total content (6:47:28), and for each of the topics, it breaks out the sub-topics! In this screenshot, we see six broad topics, and we see the sub-topics under Welcome and Meditation. (There was not room in the screenshot to open up all six, but you get the idea.)

I'm probably sounding like a broken record by now, but again – what we do NOT want to do is reinvent the wheel. We want to model what works. So, we now have literally every key element of the best-selling meditation course in the marketplace broken down for us in detail and in plain sight.

It still blows my mind sometimes that this information is freely available. But what blows my mind even more? How few people know about it. And even among those who do, almost no one analyzes it from a business and marketing perspective like we're doing. You have a *ridiculous* unfair advantage here. Use it!

You may not realize it yet, but trust me when I say that you are already so far ahead of the curve, it isn't even funny!

3D Glasses Tool #3: Amazon

Back in the day, Amazon used to be pretty much all about books. The talk was whether or not it would put Barnes & Noble out of business. Now, of course, Amazon is a marketplace where you can buy, well, just about everything.

Amazon is a godsend when it comes to shopping (hello, one click Amazon Prime!). But in some ways, it's almost *too* scattered, which is why I rate Udemy slightly higher as a research tool. Still, though, Amazon is extremely valuable. Let's look at the results that are generated when we put "meditation" into the Amazon search box, and talk about what they mean and what you can do with 'em. ☺

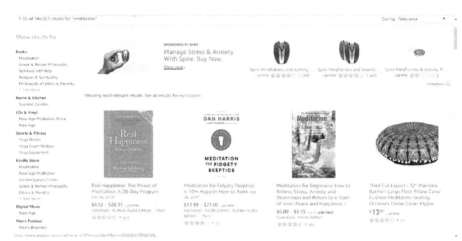

Lots of interesting stuff here. Let's start to unpack it. For my money, the most valuable aspect of Amazon as an Ultimate Vida 3D Glasses tool is to generate potential product ideas. You can see evidence of this in the left column. We've got the following sub-categories of meditation related products for sale: Books, Home & Kitchen, CDs & Vinyl, Sports & Fitness, Digital Music, and Men's Fashion. And that's only six out of 35 categories! (Below, there's a link that says "See all 35 Departments.")

Again, so far, we're still in the evaluation stage. We're not yet thinking about what kinds of products and services we might offer. That said, it's good to know that we have lots of options! It used to be tough to sell physical products online if you didn't have a warehousing and fulfillment operation set up. That's no longer the case. With the evolution and ease of drop-shipping, wholesale suppliers, and even partnering with Amazon itself, it's now easier than ever to sell physical products online as well as digital.

The reason this is important is because it's very difficult to have a profitable business with only one product. Ideally, you're going to want to have a suite of products to offer, to appeal to different segments of the market, and at different price points.

That said, do NOT get intimidated or overwhelmed by this. First of all, you won't have to house inventory, as mentioned. And second? There are also ways to make money from a market without even selling any products at all! It's all possible, so take a deep breath, and let's keep exploring. ☺

I won't go into too much more depth about the Amazon screenshot above, because the rest of it is fairly similar to Udemy. That said, Amazon is obviously a much larger marketplace than Udemy, so it can be useful to validate your Udemy findings on Amazon. The way you'd want to do that is again look at the customer reviews and:

1. Look for the products with the most reviews, as this means they're also the products with the most buyers.

2. Look for the products with the highest ratings, as these are the ones you'll want to model and pay closer attention to.

3. Within the reviews of the highest-rated products, read through the positive reviews as well as the negative ones, to identify key points to include as well as key mistakes to avoid. Again, this applies no matter what kind of solution you eventually offer, so don't worry about that part yet.

Once you apply 3D Glasses Tools 1, 2, and 3, you should have a pretty badass research file that gives you a serious unfair advantage over others in the space. But if you think it's been good so far? Well, as the famous song and saying goes… "You ain't seen nothing yet." Without further ado, I present to you…

3D Glasses Tool #4: Facebook Audience Insights (AKA the Motherlode!)

So, here's the deal. Everyone knows about Facebook (duh). Some people even know about Facebook Audience Insights. But almost no one fully understands the immense power of this tool and how to leverage it.

What I'm about to share with you has blown away even **8-figure business owners and multi-millionaires whom I've shown it to**. So pay close attention. ☺

Oh, and as always, my promise to keep things timeless stands. If this tool ever goes away or becomes less valuable, or if a better one emerges that achieves the same goal, you'll always know about it at:

www.UltimateVida. com/toolbox.

With that said, let's dive in! For starters, the URL for Facebook Audience Insights (which you'll want to bookmark and add to your shortcuts!) is:

https://www.facebook.com/ads/audience-insights

Keep in mind that you'll have to be logged into your (or any) Facebook account for it to load properly. If you have any issues (or if Facebook changes that URL), just Google "Facebook Audience Insights" and it should come up there as well. The welcome screen should look like this:

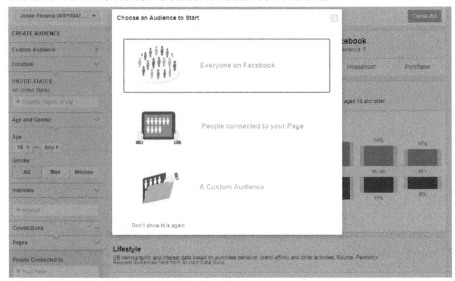

Go ahead and select "Everyone on Facebook" to get started. And also set the location to United States, if it doesn't come up as the default. Do this even if you're not in the United States – I'll explain why in a moment.

OK, now let's get started. See that white box in the left column that says "Interests?" That's where we're going to start by entering the broad category of whichever space we're researching, and go from there. It's part art and part science. Here's how I'd break it down, continuing with the meditation example.

Step 1: Type "meditation" into the search box, but don't actually make a selection yet, and see what related terms Facebook suggests:

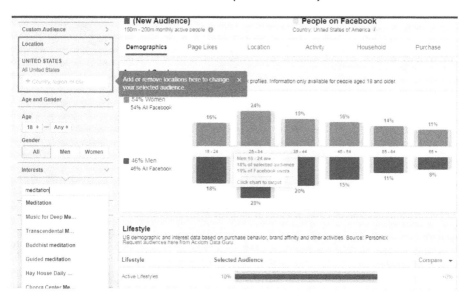

So, here's the deal. By this point in the process, you would have already gone through UV 3D Glasses Tools 1, 2, and 3 (Forums, Udemy & Amazon), and started to at least slightly narrow down a broad category into some sub-segments. If this isn't clear to you, circle back and re-read these three sections.

The basic idea is that trying to be all things to all people rarely works in any market. Ideally, you want to "go deep" instead of "go wide" and talk to a segment of the market (that your research shows are likely buyers) in a very intimate way.

So, in the case of meditation, this segmentation could zero in on a certain form of meditation, such as Vipassana (like we examined in the forums). Or it could hone in on a certain type of person (i.e. meditation for entrepreneurs, or meditation for moms).

Just for argument's sake, let's say our research had revealed "Transcendental Meditation" to be a strong-looking sub-niche within the meditation category. We would then select it from the suggestions or just type it in, and our results would look like this (note: if your research has already revealed more specific search terms, by all means type them straight into the interest box instead of the broad term):

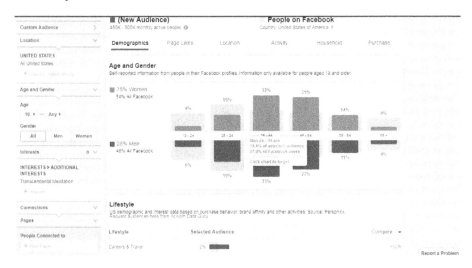

OK, lots to unpack here, so let's jump right in! The first thing we always want to look at is the audience size, which is listed at the top. See where it says 450-500k monthly active people? This means that there are between 450,000 and 500,000 people in the United States interested in transcendental meditation. For reference, we can compare this to the previous screenshot, which has 150-200 million active people (note: this was with NO targeting, which simply means that there are 150-200 million active Facebook users in the U.S.

Moving on... see how there are six tabs at the top of the page? That's already been changed — Facebook is always moving, which is why I always focus on timeless strategies rather than short term tricks — as I write this, there are now only four tabs at the top of the page! So, right now, we're in the "demographics" tab, which is underlined. That's where we always want to start, to get a basic snapshot of this segment and take their pulse.

Here we see that 75% of this segment are women, and almost 2/3 of these women (63% to be exact) are between the ages of 25 and 44. So at first glance, this appears to be our "sweet spot." But we're not doing anything with this info just yet, other than noting it in our research file, either by adding in the data, or just taking a screenshot.

Next, we want to scroll down to look at the "Lifestyle" section, and make sure the data is sorted by the "Compare" column on the right.

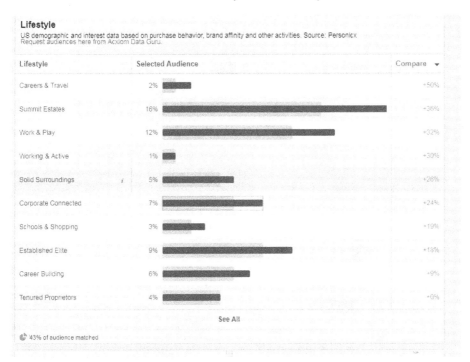

In this screenshot, the middle column represents the proportion of your audience that falls into this category, relative to all Facebook users. For example, in the top-listed lifestyle, "Careers & Travel," 2% of people into transcendental meditation fall into this lifestyle category, and you can see that this is quite a bit more likely than Facebook users in general. In addition to the percentages, you can read this data visually, as the dark blue bar will always represent your audience, while the lighter bar represents Facebook users on the whole. It can also be useful to sort this middle column by size to simply find out which lifestyle groups make up the largest portions of your audience.

Next, we have the Compare column, which in my opinion is even more important. For example, we see here that the transcendental meditation crowd is 50% more likely to be in the "Careers & Travel" lifestyle than the average Facebook user. The reason this is so important is that we want to understand at a deep, intimate level who we're talking to, what their lives look like, and how to best communicate with them.

To that end, it's obviously crucial that we understand exactly what each of these lifestyle groups actually means! To do that, we simply hover our mouse next to any group for which we want an explanation. For example:

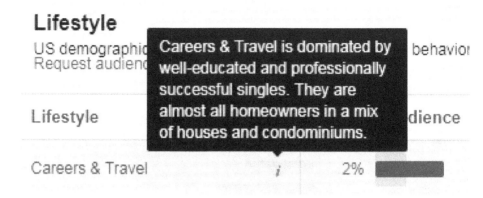

These black boxes are your friends! They are a treasure trove of valuable information. But the key here is that we want to make sure we're taking an accurate pulse of the market. So, while Careers & Travel is the top-rated lifestyle in terms of affinity (the "compare" column), we also need to be aware that it only represents 2% of this particular market (transcendental meditation).

So, we also want to sort the data by the middle column. As you can see, it's called "Selected Audience." But I simply call it "size." And in this case, size most definitely matters! When we do this, here's what we get:

The key point to note here is that our top two lifestyle categories – Summit Estates and Work & Play – also have positive compare scores. This means that people who are into transcendental meditation are 36% and 33% more likely, respectively, to fall into these categories than the average Facebook user. The third highest lifestyle category by size, on the other hand (Firmly Established) has a negative affinity score, so I wouldn't place too much emphasis on it.

Now we'd want to dig a bit deeper and look for common trends and themes. The way we'd do that is by opening up our little black box friends next to Summit Estates and Work & Play, and seeing what (if anything) they might have in common!

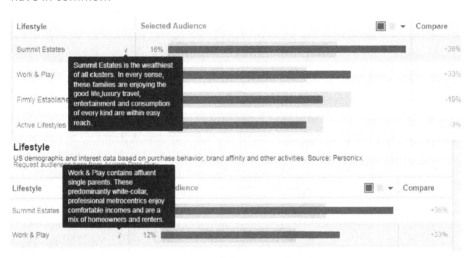

Right away, we see one major common element between these two lifestyles that's practically screaming at us. Just in these two little black boxes, we see:

- "Wealthiest of all clusters"
- Good life
- Luxury travel
- Entertainment and consumption of every king
- Within "easy reach"
- Affluent
- White-collar
- Comfortable incomes

So, let's see…do you think wealth and financial stability might just be a hallmark of transcendental meditators? And do you think it might be a good thing that your audience has disposable income (extra money) to spend on things they're passionate about? ☺

Aside from their economic status, we see that one category consists mostly of families, while the other is predominantly single parents. So, what I'd do here is note that parents *might* be a theme here, but it's not nearly as overwhelming as the financial aspect.

Hopefully it's starting to make sense how we analyze this data to begin to form a snapshot of who we're speaking to here. The idea is to connect with them on a very intimate level. Make them feel like we really "get them." And this information helps us do that.

Think of each data point here as one piece of the puzzle. Which brings us to the next pieces of said puzzle, as we stay within the demographics tab and scroll down the page to the next three areas we want to look at: relationship status, education level and job status.

What we're looking for here are significant, eye-popping trends. These trends are again expressed by the red and green "affinity scores." We want to note if there are any substantial positive or negative trends in these categories among the audience we're analyzing.

Starting with relationship status, nothing major jumps out at me here. The percentage of both married and single people in this audience mirrors the general population very closely, as evidenced by their affinity scores of 2% and 5%. The "in a relationship" and "engaged" options are slightly negative, but not by a very high percentage, nor do they make up a big segment of this market.

As we move on to "Education Level," things begin to get more interesting. We see that our audience is far less likely (48%) to have only a high school education than Facebook users in general. This is further confirmed and then some by noting that our audience is over twice as likely (110%) to have a graduate school degree than all of Facebook users!

So now our audience is beginning to take shape as highly educated and financially well off. Now let's look at the final field in this tab, "Job Title," and see what we find...

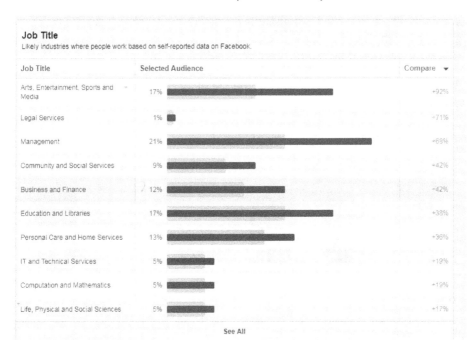

Job Title
Likely industries where people work based on self-reported data on Facebook.

Job Title	Selected Audience	Compare ▾
Arts, Entertainment, Sports and Media	17%	+92%
Legal Services	1%	+71%
Management	21%	+68%
Community and Social Services	9%	+42%
Business and Finance	12%	+42%
Education and Libraries	17%	+38%
Personal Care and Home Services	13%	+36%
IT and Technical Services	5%	+19%
Computation and Mathematics	5%	+19%
Life, Physical and Social Sciences	5%	+17%

See All

Now in all candor, I find that the Job Title section is often not as useful as some of the others. But still, sometimes there are some gold nuggets here. Just as we did with Lifestyle, here we want to look for job titles that represent both a healthy size of our audience, and a strong positive affinity score. It looks like the following job titles are the ones that fit the bill:

- Arts, Entertainment, Sports & Media (way too broad, if you ask me!)
- Management
- Business and Finance
- Education and Libraries
- Personal Care and Home Services

As I suspected, not an overwhelming amount of useful info or commonalities here, but still worth noting. Why is it worth noting, despite these job titles not having too much in common? Well... let me plant a seed here for you. In addition to our primary purpose of this research – getting to know our audience on a personal, intimate level – we may also want to advertise to them at some point. And knowing which sub-segments of our audience are likely to be most receptive to our message is a huge competitive advantage that we may want to leverage. ☺

The Art of Freedom

We have now completed our analysis of the "Demographics" tab! If you're going through this exercise with one of your own ideas/markets, your research file should be rapidly expanding with valuable info. Yes, or yes? ☺

Moving right along, we click over to the "Activity" tab and here's what we get:

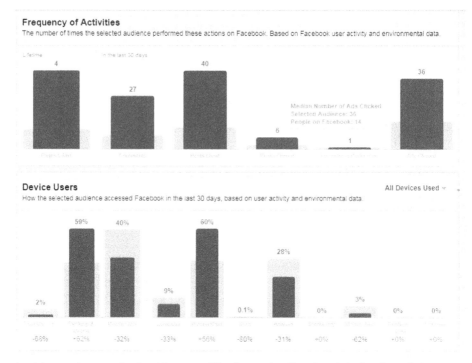

In this section, we're looking specifically at the Facebook behavior of the users in this group (transcendental meditation). In a broader sense, this gives insights as to how they behave online in a social media or community setting related to this particular topic.

The data in the top section – Frequency of Activities – is some of the strongest, most overwhelming and encouraging data that we've seen thus far. Just from a quick glance, we can see that these users are FAR more active and engaged than the average Facebook user, as they have executed several times as many likes, shares and comments. Just to be clear, the dark bars always represent the segment we're looking at, while the lighter bars represent Facebook users on the whole.

If we hover our mouse over any of the specific activities, we can see the exact breakdown. I have done this with the "Ads clicked" activity above to illustrate the point. It's no accident that I picked this particular activity, as "ads clicked" is the most important part of this graphic in my opinion. The reason for this is that it helps to know that, if we eventually run some form of advertising in this market, the people are likely to be receptive. Above we can see that while the average Facebook user clicked 14 ads in the past 30 days, our audience clicked 36. Calculated another way, this says that our audience is a whopping 157% more likely to click on ads than the average Facebook user. That's a massive positive factor which bodes very well.

The bottom section of the Activity tab – Device Users – can also be very revealing. For obvious reasons, it is super important to know where your market is likely to access their information, and to ensure that the presentation of your content and marketing message is compatible with that platform. Note that this data can vary wildly depending on the topic, age group, education level, and other factors of your audience.

Two significant data points jump out at me in this particular case:

First, we see that this market is 59% more likely than the average Facebook user to access info via both desktop and mobile. This is worth noting, as an increasing number of users in various markets are moving towards mobile only, and it's obviously a very different user experience to access content on a phone vs. a desktop computer.

The second – and even more notable – point that jumps out at me is that our audience is 56% more likely to use an iphone/ipad, and 31% less likely to use an Android than the general population. It may seem overly granular to get into which specific device a person is using, but I assure you it's not. I have bought millions and millions of dollars of media online and many of my campaigns have shown a significant difference in performance from one device to another. So, it stands to reason that, when you eventually reach the stage of being ready to monetize a certain market, your user experience is optimized for the devices where your people are most likely to consume their content.

Now, as we move to the "Location" tab, it's time to "go global!" This is always one of my favorite parts of analyzing an audience. But before we do, we've got to make one critical change to the data. So far, all of our analysis has been for the U.S. portion of our audience only. The main reason for that is because much of the data we've been looking at is only available in the U.S. (Some of it has just recently been made available in a few other countries such as the U.K. and Australia too, but it's still not available in most of the world.)

For the last two portions of our analysis, though, we're going to remove the U.S.-only parameter, and look at this audience worldwide. When we do that, here's what we get:

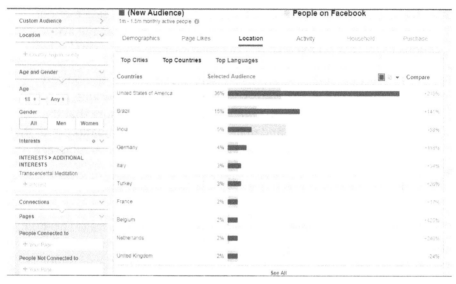

The first thing to note here is the change to the audience size. Remember when we started with the U.S. only, the audience size was 450k – 500k people? Now, if we look at the top of this graphic, we can see that we've got between 1 and 1.5 million people. So, the audience triples as we go worldwide. Not surprising, but still exciting!

Now, as always, we can sort by either size of the audience (middle column) or the positive/negative affinity score (right column). For the location analysis, unless the audience is enormous (10 million or more), I usually start by sorting by size. To illustrate why I do this, let's take Belgium for example (third from the bottom). It's got a crazy high compare score (425%). Normally I'd get very excited by this, but in this case my excitement is tempered by the fact that it only makes up 2% of this particular market. So while these 20,000 or so people may be very interested, they're a very small portion of the audience and therefore saturation will inevitably happen quickly. Not to mention the language barrier, which we'll get into in a moment.

So, back to size. Size matters, remember? What we're looking for here are countries that make up a good chunk of our audience, **and** have a high affinity score. These countries tend to be our "sweet spot." In this case, the

U.S. certainly qualifies, as does Brazil. These two countries make up 35% and 15% of the market, respectively, and have very strong affinity scores of 218% and 141%!

Note: literally every time I do this analysis, I am completely surprised with some of what I find. For example, if you had asked me before I pulled up this data whether Brazil or India had more people into transcendental meditation, I would have said India without hesitation. But I would have been completely wrong. Not only does Brazil make up a larger portion of the market, it is *three times* as large, despite India having a far greater population! And furthermore, has a much higher affinity score, while India actually has a negative affinity score! That's why doing this analysis is so important. We as humans have our perceptions and beliefs – some warranted, some not. But the data never lies. The data gives us the actual truth and reality of a given group of people's actions and behaviors. And that's always what we want to base our decisions on.

What's also useful to do here is take our geo-analysis one level deeper, and look at the city breakdown. When we do this, here's what we find:

The Art of Freedom

There are several key data points that jump out here:

- I've done hundreds of these analyses, and it's incredibly rare for the top 10 cities by size to all have positive affinity scores. In this case, my theory as to why is because with the exception of Istanbul and Rome, these cities are either in the U.S. or Brazil, and both countries seem to be hyper-interested in transcendental meditation.

- Even though the U.S. makes up a considerably larger portion of the audience than Brazil (35% vs. 15%), our top two cities by size are both in Brazil – Sao Paulo and Rio de Janeiro. Not only that, but the affinity scores for these two cities are insanely high (683% and 567%!).

- This data also strongly tells us that if we want to market to this audience in the U.S., we might want to start with New York, Los Angeles and Chicago.

Are you starting to see the immense power of this data and how little by little, piece by piece, it literally gives us a road map for how and where to approach any given audience? And in case you're thinking this is sneaky or nefarious in some way, it's actually quite the opposite. This data shows us exactly how to approach an audience in ways that they're most likely to appreciate and be receptive to.

Let's take a look at the final subsection in the Location tab – language:

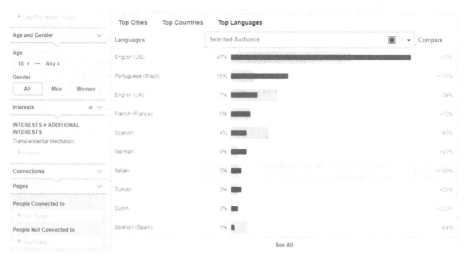

No big surprise here; English and Portuguese (Brazil's national language) are the two most prominent languages in this space. But here's a subtle point that you may not have noticed at first glance. See how "U.S. English" has a 53% positive affinity score? That's quite a bit lower than the striking 218%

affinity score for the U.S. overall! What does this mean? Well... that a big part of the difference between 53% and 218% is likely due to people in the U.S. who speak other languages! Which language could be the main factor here? You guessed it – Portuguese!

Now, here's where we need to do some strategic and cost/benefit analysis. I say that because, if I look at this data in a vacuum, it would seem like a no-brainer to eventually have whatever content we produce translated to Portuguese and enter the Brazilian market. But while translation is easier today than it's ever been, it's still a task. So I'd probably want to first validate whatever business plan we eventually come up with (more on this in the following chapters) in English. But if we successfully do that? We'd want to move into Brazil and Portuguese very soon thereafter.

Are you seeing how this gets very fun and exciting, creating these global online businesses, seemingly out of thin air? If it still seems fuzzy to you, have no fear, soon it will all become far clearer. In fact, I think that's going to happen starting right now. Because if you've found this analysis revealing so far? Forget about 3D glasses. Now we're going to put on **4D** glasses – because I'm about to show you the mother lode of the mother lode! What I'm referring to, of course, is the last tab of our Audience Insights analysis: Page likes. Let's dive right in.

Note: in this case, it is important to click the "See All" link below #10 as many times as you're able to, so that you'll be able to see all the available data.

11	Interest	Abraham-Hicks • Doreen Virtue • NaturalNews.com
12	Musician/Band	Music for Deep Meditation
13	News & Media Website	Conscious Life News • mindbodygreen
14	Entertainment Website	The Earth Tribe • Earth. We are one.
15	Charity Organization	Humanity Healing
16	Author	Pema Chodron • Eckhart Tolle • Deepak Chopra • Thich Nhat Hanh
17	Organization	Wild Woman Sisterhood
18	Education Website	Expanded Consciousness
19	TV Show	SuperSoul
20	Public Figure	Marianne Williamson • Energy Therapy • Healing Light • Tony Robbins
21	Food & Beverage Company	Traditional Medicinals
22	Magazine	Mother Earth News • Yoga Journal • Vegetarian Times
23	Social Media Agency	Universe Explorers
24	Media	I'm not "Spiritual." I just practice being a good person. • Truth Theory • Green Renaissance
25	Writer	Elizabeth Gilbert
26	Community	Meditation Masters • Manifesting - The Law of Attraction & The Secret
27	Media/News Company	Hay House • Elephant Meditation • Elephant Journal • Yoga International
28	Art	Educate Inspire Change
29	Scientist	Nikola Tesla
30	Personal Blog	Herbs, Health and Happiness
31	Environmental Conservation Organization	The Rainforest Site

Here's what we get in this case:

It would be hard for me to overstate how incredibly valuable this information is. Corporations literally shell out millions of dollars in market research and "focus group" studies to acquire this kind of data.

Among the many gems of data we get here include:

- Their favorite meditation centers
- Their most visited websites
- Their primary educational resources
- Their most-consumed products & services

- Their favorite movies, tv shows and musicians
- Where they consume their news & media
- The non-profits they're most likely to donate to
- Their favorite authors, scientist & public figures
- Their most-read blogs and magazines
- Their most trusted media & news companies

When you go through this analysis for your own ideas and potential markets/ audiences, make sure to pay attention to each and every category listed here, no matter how innocuous it may seem.

There are two main reasons why this analysis is so important, and in my view is the most valuable tab that Audience Insights has to offer:

First, as I mentioned before, it's crucial to develop a closer, more intimate understanding of who these people are and what makes them tick. You want to connect with them on a genuine, human level. And if you think about it, knowing their tendencies and preferences in the areas above, combined with all of the demographic and quantitative data we've already uncovered, will help you do just that. I mean, do you even know all of this information about your friends and family? Yeah, me neither. ☺

The second reason is that, no matter what strategy you ultimately use to enter a market, you're going to want to know where your audience hangs out online, and what they're into. And this data is pretty much a freaking treasure map that'll lead you straight to the buried jewels! Virtually each one of these 31 categories gives you laser-like targeting options that are right on point for your audience. By "targeting options," I simply mean putting your message in front of your audience. To get even more specific:

- If you want to go "organic" (i.e. free traffic rather than paid), you now know which sites, blogs, networks and media you may want to consider publishing content on.

- If you choose to go with a paid traffic strategy (the option I usually prefer – more on this soon), this data tells you exactly which keywords and websites have the best chance of converting well with your audience – both on Facebook and beyond.

In fact, if you do decide to move forward in a market after you've done your analysis, you'll want to take this personal connection even further, by creating what's called an "avatar" (more on that in a second).

For the final piece of our Audience Insights analysis, let's look at the bottom half of the Page Likes tab, and see what we get:

Page Likes
Facebook Pages that are likely to be relevant to your audience based on Facebook Page likes.

Page	Relevance *i* ▾	Audience	Facebook	Affinity *i*
Meditação Transcendental	1	80.3K	79.7K	1265x
Transcendental Meditation	2	389.3K	514.7K	950x
The Shift Network	3	52.3K	433K	152x
One Mind Dharma	4	52.2K	439.1K	149x
The Sacred Science	5	62.2K	531K	147x
Meditation Techniques	6	70.2K	621.1K	142x
Buddha Groove	7	56.1K	505.7K	139x
Soulvana	8	58K	561.2K	130x
Abraham-Hicks	9	54.4K	527.4K	130x
Hay House	10	68.2K	675.3K	127x

See More

Note: I did not click "see more" in this case, because there can often be up to 100 entries in this section, and I don't want to bombard you with graphic after graphic. But when you do this analysis for yourself, I highly recommend clicking "see all" until it's no longer an option, so that you get to access all the data.

The default sort in this case also happens to be the most important column, which is affinity. This is basically the same as the "compare" score in the previous tabs. But here's some startling perspective: Remember when we uncovered a couple of compare scores in the 500% to 600% range, and I said how remarkable it was? Well, the highest compare (affinity) score in this case is a whopping 126,500%! That's over *250 times* the highest compare score from before.

Now to be fair, the top two affinity scores here are specifically for pages related to transcendental meditation (did you notice that the top one is in Portuguese?!). But even our third-place finisher, "The Shift Network," has a

152x affinity score, which is 15,200%! Are you seeing the implications here? It's truly mind-boggling how targeted and on point these pages are. The possibilities are endless, from advertising on these pages or pages like them, reaching out to the owner and negotiating some sort of reciprocal content-sharing arrangement, etc. Tip: if you're ever unsure what a page is and whether it's relevant for you, you can always just right-click and open it up. Let's do that with the shift network, to give an example:

Above is a quick snapshot of the "Shift Network" Facebook page, which has a colossal 152x affinity score with transcendental meditation. Taking a quick glance at it, it's easy to see why. Their mission is to "lead the way to an enlightened society." Definitely very synergistic with transcendental meditation! Their cover graphic shows an upcoming event, which suggests that the page is also current and active. And when I clicked over to their "community" tab, I discovered that the page has 452,000 likes and 451,000 followers!

Want to go even further down the rabbit hole? Here's a little-known but highly valuable component of Facebook pages. If you click on the "home" tab of any Facebook page (also the default), and scroll down a bit in the right column, you'll come to a section called "pages liked by this page." When I did this with The Shift Network page, here's what came up:

These are just the first seven that popped up. There are a ton more if I keep scrolling. These are all pages that have liked the Shift Network page.

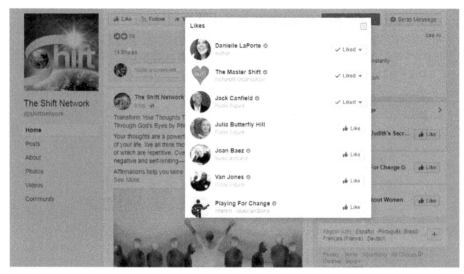

Why does that matter for you and your analysis? Because pages that have liked a certain page have a strong chance of audience overlap.

It is literally endless how far you can take this, as you can repeat this analysis with any page as the base. And I don't just mean the "page like" analysis. I'm talking the whole enchilada. For example, when I see a massively high affinity score like 152x that the shift network has with transcendental meditation, I would then go back and enter the shift network in the interest box in the left column of Audience Insights (and delete the original search) to see if it appears as an interest. Note: when I did this, it did, and it has an audience of 450-500k people and revealed a ton of interesting data in its own right!

The way I like to visualize it is as a tree.

You have your main market you're researching as the trunk or base of the tree – in this case, transcendental meditation.

You then use the demographics, purchase, household, activity and location tabs to take the pulse of this market and identify their defining characteristics.

You then use the mother lode of all tabs – Page Likes – to both amplify and crystallize their defining characteristics, and discover how to reach them online.

You then take the pages and interests in both sections of the page like tab that have the highest affinity with your root search, and if you want to take it even a step further, repeat the analysis on those — they'll become the branches of your tree.

And if you want to take it yet another level down, you can get into the branches off of the branches, etc. Literally just like a tree. This is, incidentally, also a great formula to map out seven-figure and eight-figure business plans that have little to no risk of saturation because you'll be playing chess with your marketing and targeting while everyone else is playing checkers.

By the way — step #3 from the action steps below is the SINGLE MOST IMPORTANT part of the book so far. Complete it — genuinely complete it — in the same detail and depth as I describe above — and you immediately catapult yourself to the head of the class.

I've never met anyone who has COMPLETED this step and not achieved success.

Do NOT skip it.

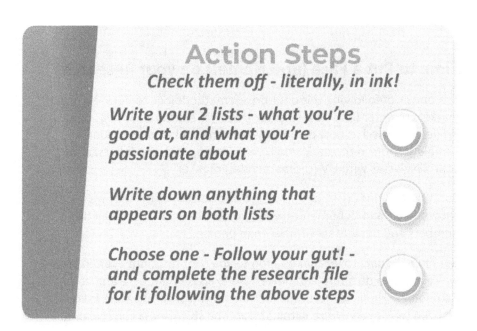

Action Steps
Check them off - literally, in ink!

Write your 2 lists - what you're good at, and what you're passionate about ◡

Write down anything that appears on both lists ◡

Choose one - Follow your gut! - and complete the research file for it following the above steps ◡

Step 6: Can You Make That Guard a Friend?

Time to Put a Face (and Name!) on your Research

The power of following this data-driven methodology to decide which markets to enter (and how to enter them!) is extraordinarily potent. While others will at best be doing guesswork and at worst taking complete shots in the dark, you'll be operating with the full vision of your 3D glasses with UV (Ultimate Vida!) rays. ☺

But if there's one "risk" of following this framework, it's that we allow the data to dehumanize what we do. That we'll be driven by numbers and percentages rather than people.

But I'm not going to let that happen to you. Not now, not ever. In fact, we're going to do a fun (and powerful!) exercise right here and now. Remember when we were kids, we had our favorite "invisible friend" who we took everywhere with us? Don't be shy, I know you had one. Well, now we're going back to our roots and we're going to create an "invisible" best friend (or two!) for you.

What I mean by this is that we're going to create an "avatar" (or two) which is a fictional character who represents your ideal customer in this market. This may sound silly, but I assure you it helps a lot and really works wonders.

This is where you take your best shot at creating a "real person" who is the most accurate representation of your audience. Give them a name. Grab or create a photo for them. The whole nine yards. I'm totally serious. I usually create two avatars – one male and one female – for any market I'm going to enter (unless, of course, I'm only targeting one gender).

Here's an example of an avatar I'd create based on the meditation research and data we just compiled:

Let's Meet Our New Best Friend, Maria

Maria is a 44-year-old executive with a prestigious, fast-paced media company in Los Angeles. She's married to Nicholas, a busy executive in his own right. Their 22-year-old son, Tyler, just graduated college and their 18-year-old daughter, Anna, just started college, so they find themselves empty nesters for the first time.

Maria has always had a spiritual inclination, and has enjoyed for quite some time reading works by luminaries such as Deepak Chopra, Louise Hay, and Elizabeth Gilbert. But while her kids were growing up in the house, it was all she could do to sneak in a few minutes of reading or yoga between her career and parenting duties. Feeling somewhat empty and restless, but also with more time on her hands now that her kids are out of the house, she starts to read about and experiment with different forms of meditation, and finds that transcendental meditation is the kind that most resonates with her.

Maria and Nicholas are financially secure and appreciate the finer things in life, and while she is professional and stylish, she is not primarily driven by money. In fact, now more than ever with her kids out of the house, she's struggling to identify her higher purpose or calling. She knows that meditation is a great foundation and is committed to making it part of her daily practice. The transcendental variety particularly appeals to her because of the anchoring technique of the consistent sound or mantra.

Maria is quite internet savvy due to her job and her natural curiosity, and would definitely be drawn to transcendental meditation programs she can access online. She also values connectivity, and with her children not consuming her energy as they used to, the idea of being part of meditation and spiritual groups and communities is very appealing to her.

"OK, So What?"

Now's where we really get to have some fun and bring your avatar to life! The first way we do this is with the "so what" method. It's really simple. Just take each data point that your research revealed, and ask yourself "so what?" As in, "so what does this mean for his/her life?"

To see how it works, let's break down my avatar for Maria in the transcendental meditation space, piece by piece. It starts like this:

Maria is a 44-year-old executive with a prestigious, fast-paced media company in Los Angeles. She's married to Nicholas, a busy executive in his own right. Their 22-year-old son, Tyler, just graduated from college and their 18-year-old daughter, Anna, just started, so they find themselves empty nesters for the first time.

You can think of the opening of your avatar as "Just the facts, ma'am." To refresh your memory, our demographic research on the transcendental meditation market showed the following:

In this case, 75% of our audience is female, and 35-44 and 45-54 run neck and neck for most likely age group, with 35-55 being slightly more likely (32% to 31%).

So, I made Maria 44 because the data showed that this is her most likely age.

Similarly, I made Maria married, simply because the data shows that this is the most likely scenario. Oh, and why did I call her Maria, and her husband

Nicholas? No scientific reason here. You get to have fun with your names. In the case of Maria, I tend to think internationally and I speak Spanish, so I went with Maria. Note, however, that despite the ambiguous heritage of the name Maria, I am not deciding that she is Latina, because I have no data to support that. If the data did show that she were Latina, I would have no problem declaring her as such, and working it into her story and identity. But that's not the case here, so let's continue...

Now, how did I decide that Maria is "an executive with a prestigious, fast-paced media company in Los Angeles?" Well, here's what our job data showed:

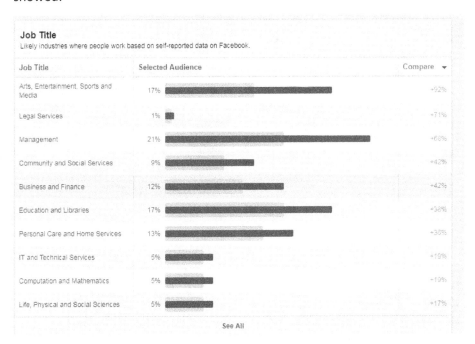

Job Title
Likely industries where people work based on self-reported data on Facebook.

Job Title	Selected Audience		Compare ▼
Arts, Entertainment, Sports and Media	17%		+92%
Legal Services	1%		+71%
Management	21%		+68%
Community and Social Services	9%		+42%
Business and Finance	12%		+42%
Education and Libraries	17%		+38%
Personal Care and Home Services	13%		+38%
IT and Technical Services	5%		+19%
Computation and Mathematics	5%		-19%
Life, Physical and Social Sciences	5%		+17%

See All

The three most likely job categories here, based on size of the market are:

- Management (21%)

- Arts, entertainment, sports & media (17%); and

- Education and Libraries (17%)

However, of these three, Arts, entertainment, sports & media has the highest affinity score by far (92%). Again, this means that people into transcendental meditation are 92% more likely than the general public to have a career in this area.

Now, how did I decide that Maria and her family live in L.A.? Well, on a country level, the data shows that the U.S. has by far the highest share of this market (36%). No major surprise there. And when we drill down to the city level, the data shows the following:

First things first. I was seriously tempted to make Maria Brazilian! (Side note: Isn't this fun, getting to create these characters and bringing them to life? ☺) Right?! I mean, the data supports it and then some. Sao Paulo has over twice the market share of any city in the world, AND has the highest affinity score, at a whopping 683%! And in second place is Rio!

I ultimately decided against making her Brazilian (for now). Mainly for the practical reason that I don't speak Portuguese and it would be a bit more challenging to get things translated, etc. Certainly not insurmountable, but given that the U.S. dominates market share and also has a high affinity score, my choice here is to see if I can first "prove the concept" in English.

But if I can? You better believe that I'll quickly pivot to the Brazilian market. In fact, this sounds like lots of fun! Plus, from a business standpoint, it's wiser positioning to be a "big fish in a smaller pond." (Fun fact: Google "most common female names in Brazil" and let me know what you come up with. ☺

OK, back to the present. Now that we've decided we're starting in the U.S., why L.A.? Well, the data above shows that New York, L.A. and Chicago are the top three cities for this market in terms of size. All three enjoy a very strong affinity score. Of the three, L.A. ranks the highest with 550%, which starts to shift things in its favor. But what really seals the deal for me is that I lived in the L.A. area for many years. So I'm very familiar with the southern California coastal lifestyle. Don't be afraid to pull your own life experience into the mix when creating your avatars! As long as the data supports it, it's a very smart move that will make everything you do more effective because it's based in reality!

So, how do we work the "So what?" framework into our avatar, making him or her more human? Well, we start adding in life and personality and color. But the key is logical color. Plausible color. For example:

Fact: Maria's two children are now both out of the house

Result: Maria and her husband Nicholas are now "empty nesters" for the first time

So what?

- How is Maria likely to feel?
- How would you feel in a similar major life-changing event?
- Would you feel restless? Anxious? Uneasy?
- Maybe even on the verge of a mid-life crisis?
- But perhaps also excited and curious about what you can now create?
- Maybe even playful? Stoking your inner child?

Suddenly, Maria feels like a real person, right? Like someone you can relate to. Like someone you could hang out with, and have a LOT to talk about.

Continuing down the "so what" rabbit hole... Maria is at a crossroads in her life and feels this swirl of mixed emotions... so what? So, maybe it's time to get back to her roots. Back to her interests, hobbies and passions in life — everything that had taken a back burner to her career and raising her family. But which interests are these?

We don't just make up random ones. We take it from what the data shows us:

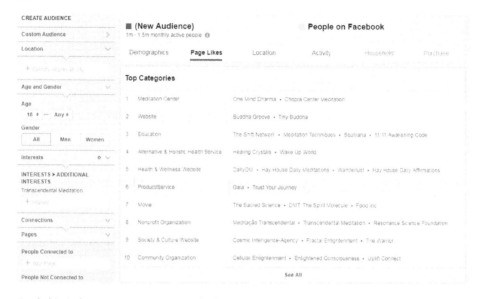

And this is how we come up with the next paragraph of our avatar:

Maria has always had a spiritual inclination, and has for quite a time enjoyed reading works by luminaries such as Deepak Chopra, Louise Hay, and Elizabeth Gilbert. But while her kids were growing up in the house, it was all she could do to sneak in a few minutes of reading or yoga between her career and parenting duties. Feeling somewhat empty and restless, but also with more time on her hands now that her kids are out of the house, she starts to read about and experiment with different forms of meditation, and finds that transcendental meditation is the kind that most resonates with her.

So now that we've anchored where Maria is at in her life... revealed some of her interests and innermost emotions... again, we ask ourselves, "So what?" In other words, "OK, that's great, but what comes next? Does she have the resources to enroll in solutions that are of interest to her?" And we continue...

Maria and Nicholas are financially secure and appreciate the finer things in life, and while she is professional and stylish, she is not primarily driven by money. In fact, now more than ever with her kids out of the house, she's struggling to identify her higher purpose or calling. She knows that meditation is a great daily foundation and is committed to making it part of her daily practice. The transcendental variety particularly appeals to her because of the anchoring technique of the consistent sound or mantra.

Maria is quite internet savvy due to her job and her natural curiosity, and would definitely be drawn to transcendental meditation programs she can access online. She also values connectivity, and with her children not consuming her energy as they used to, the idea of being part of meditation and spiritual groups and communities is very appealing to her.

Notice that we deduced a couple of things from the data, and took a bit of a poetic license, albeit a highly plausible one. Based on her job, where she lives, and the "page like" data, we can see that while Maria is not wildly rich, she's not struggling either. She and Nicholas have means. Note that this is generally a key factor you'll be looking for, unless you plan to offer a highly discounted or inexpensive solution.

And by the very nature of being interested in transcendental meditation, we intuit Maria's "higher calling." We admittedly take a bit of a leap by saying that the idea of meditation and spiritual groups and communities appeal to her. But this brings up an important point. Do we know for sure that Maria wants this? Of course not.

But here's the key point: You always want to make your avatar into a highly likely and qualified prospect for your topic and what you will eventually offer.

You're never going to appeal to everyone in your market, and that's OK. Appealing to everyone is not even an advisable goal. Remember earlier in the book, we revealed that all members of your audience are *not* created equal, and your job is to appeal to the most **obsessively passionate** ones? With that in mind, you want to mold your avatar into your "hottest prospect" most likely to take action, and then treat him/her like family or a best friend and shower them with love and value.

The idea is for your avatar to feel extremely human to you — every time you communicate to your audience, whether in writing, video or any other format, imagine yourself having drinks with your avatar who is your brother, sister or best friend, and write or talk exactly as you would over those drinks. Note the other powerful thing this avatar creation does? It once again eliminates the need for you to suddenly be an expert marketer or writer. You're quite simply being conversational and communicating in a friendly, down to earth manner, just as you would over those drinks...

1. To quickly review: In order to paint a more complete and human picture of your avatar, take each data point and ask yourself "So what?" In

other words, what does this mean? Do this with age, relationship status, frustrations, everything. There's no right or wrong answer – it doesn't have to be perfect, it just has to be human and believable.

2. Imagine yourself meeting for drinks with your avatar. What would he or she be talking about?

Remember the following and you'll do just fine: Relationship first, topic second. Say what? It's like this...

Sure, your topic is important. Extremely important, in fact. That's why we've devoted so many pages and tactics to making sure you choose a hot topic that people are actually interested in. But the key word here is **people**. Remember that at the other end of anything you write or say or do is always a person. A person just like your avatar. A person who IS your avatar. A person whose personal life and emotions always come first.

What do I mean by this?

Well, let's take our friend Maria. Sure, she's into transcendental meditation. And coming around to that is very important – after all, it's the basis of a tribe we'd build and monetize using this example. But guess what Maria's always gonna be more concerned with than meditation? M-A-R-I-A. Her SELF. Her family. Her own life. Nicholas, Anna & Tyler. Her growing restlessness and uncertainty about what the next chapter of her life will look like. So any talk of meditation (or whatever the topic of your tribe is) always must be worked in in a very human way that goes to the core of who the person is you're talking to.

Imagine you were going out for drinks with your best friend, and you both happened to be wine enthusiasts. Would you greet your friend by saying "Hey, let me tell you about the 35% discount for today only on the 2009 Chateau de la Huste Fronsac Bordeaux I just tried?" No. That would be weird, awkward and icky. I mean, you might do that like one out of every 10 times if you were excited or happy or hyper. But that wouldn't be your standard intro, would it? You'd probably first ask your friend something about their life. Or maybe share something about yours.

Note I didn't say friend in this example. I said *best* friend. Because that's how you want to think of your tribe. As your best friends, or even your family. Meaning you shouldn't be afraid of being open and transparent and vulnerable about your own personal life, just as you would with friends or family. I'm not saying be someone you're not. If you're naturally shy and reserved, fine, be yourself. But make sure they know that this is your personality. Better yet, reveal some of your insecurities relating to this.

The cliché "People don't care how much you know until they know how much you care" rings very true here. Don't be in such a hurry to teach a lesson or talk about your topic all the time. Just treat 'em like family, treat 'em with love, and believe me – when you create that kind of unbreakable bond with your tribe? You'll be able to make whatever offers you want and not only will they be wide open to them, but they'll be grateful to you for letting them know. Because *they trust you, and they see you like family, too.*

Another useful exercise to feel closer still to your tribe and avatar?

Ask yourself who your avatar might remind you of in real life? Is it your brother or sister? Or perhaps a close friend? Also, what fictional character might your avatar remind you of? Perhaps a character in a movie or a TV series you've always identified with? Think about the hit show "Friends" and how close we felt to Chandler, Joey, Monica, Phoebe, Rachel & Ross. We could totally imagine sharing a coffee and a laugh with them at Central Perk, right? Talking about everything and nothing at once. That's exactly the vibe we want to cultivate here.

And whether you're picturing a real person in your life or a character you like, picture them vividly. Picture their facial expressions, laugh, gestures etc. and imagine what you'd be saying and how you'd be acting if they were across from you. And then communicate with your tribe exactly like that, whether in writing, on video or however you choose to do it.

Action Steps

Check them off - literally, in ink!

List 5 key facts about your
avatar (based on the data)

Write down someone (real or
fictional) your avatar reminds
you of

Name your avatar, and describe
him/her - get within 20% of the
length of my model for you

Step 7: Knowing Everybody's Routine

4D Glasses Tool to Give You a *Major* Unfair Advantage

There's another incredibly powerful tool which I purposely haven't shared with you until now. But trust me, you'll want to be sitting down for this one, because it's another gem and powerhouse.

First, though, I want you to promise that you'll only use this for good. I'm being totally serious. This tool exposes some highly valuable data of successful websites (that the site owners would prefer remain hidden!), and never under any circumstances do we copy what others are doing or try to harm their businesses in any way. We only do this competitive research and put on these "3D" and "4D" glasses in order to improve our own chances of success and be of value and service in the marketplace.

The main purpose of this tool is to find out where the main players in your market are getting their website traffic from, and to reverse engineer their business model, in a sense. Again, not so you can copy, but rather to get a sense of what's working, and model success while adding your own unique twist. That approach will always give you a better chance of succeeding than trying to come up with something revolutionary.

Without further ado, the name of this tool is SimilarWeb, and the website is www.similarweb.com. This is the best tool of its kind at the time of this book's publication, but as always, my pledge to provide a timeless framework and give you the most up to date resources stands, and if a better tool becomes available, I'll share it with you at www.UltimateVida.com/toolbox.

The reason I saved this tool for last is because I really only recommend using it once you've made a final decision that you're going to enter a market. The idea is to use forums, Udemy, Amazon, and Facebook Audience Insights to make that decision. And then once it's a yes, move on to SimilarWeb. The purpose of SimilarWeb is not to confirm or validate your decision, but to take your competitive research to the next level and begin to brainstorm potential traffic sources and business models.

With that said, let's jump in. ☺

Now, obviously, for SimilarWeb to have any value or purpose, you have to know which websites to enter and analyze. Fear not, I've got you covered. We're going to draw from three sources:

- If you happen to know any of the major players in the space based on your knowledge, research or connections (if so, note down the URLs of their sites).

- Any major sites or audiences that came up in your 3D glasses research tools, now is the time to enter them in to see what they're up to and what their model looks like. Note: this is also the time to use good ol' Google to see if any of the large Facebook audiences (that you uncovered in the "Page Likes" tab of Facebook Audience Insights) have websites we can analyze.

- Speaking of Google; if you are still unclear on the major players in this space – or even if you are – now is the time to figure out who they are. The way we do this is as simple and basic as it gets. We simply go to Google and enter in our main search term (in this case, "transcendental meditation:"

Once we scroll past the sponsored listings (don't worry, we'll get into the ad side of things very soon), here are the first few results:

Transcendental Meditation (TM) Technique - Newport Beach - TM.org
https://www.tm.org/transcendental-meditation-coastal-orange-county ▼
Learn the Transcendental Meditation technique from a Certified Teacher in Newport Beach, Costa Mesa,
Huntington Beach, Coastal Orange County. Costa.

Transcendental Meditation - Wikipedia
https://en.wikipedia.org/wiki/Transcendental_Meditation ▼
Transcendental Meditation (TM) refers to a specific form of silent mantra meditation called the
Transcendental Meditation technique, and less commonly to the organizations that constitute the
Transcendental Meditation movement. Maharishi Mahesh Yogi (1918–2008) introduced the TM
technique and TM movement in ...
Meditation technique · History of Transcendental ... Maharishi Foundation
You've visited this page 3 times. Last visit: 1/14/18

Transcendental Meditation: Benefits, Technique, and More - WebMD
https://www.webmd.com › Health & Balance › Guide ▼
Oct 29, 2017 · Transcendental Meditation (TM) is a technique for avoiding distracting thoughts and
promoting a state of relaxed awareness. The late Maharishi Mahesh Yogi derived TM from the ancient
Vedic tradition of India. He brought the technique to the U.S. in the 1960s. While meditating, the person
practicing TM ...

Transcendental Meditation: A quick introduction - TMhome
https://tmhome.com/transcendental-meditation/ ▼
An overview of what the Transcendental Meditation practice (TM) is and is not: 1. ORIGINS, 2.
BENEFITS, 3. TECHNIQUE & MANTRAS, 4. COST.

About TM - David Lynch Foundation
https://www.davidlynchfoundation.org/about-tm.html ▼
It changed my life. "Meditation has changed my life. It makes me calm and happy – and it gives me
some peace and quiet in what's a pretty chaotic life!" – Hugh Jackman. video What Is TM? with Bob
Roth. video Jerry Seinfeld: "It's like a charger for your body and mind." video Ellen DeGeneres "It gives me
a peacefulness

From a quick glance, it appears that tm.org and tmhome.com may be central
or foundational sites in this space. It also appears that David Lynch is a
key figure in this space. (When I scrolled down beyond this screenshot, he
appeared in a second listing on the first page of results.)

So now let's head over to SimilarWeb and punch
in the first site – tm.org – and see what we get:

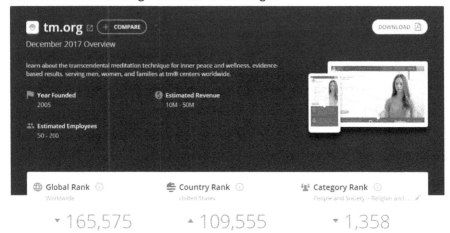

BOOM! I don't want to jump the gun, but at first glance, it appears that we have seriously hit the jackpot! This company is estimated to have revenues between $10 million and $50 million per year! I'd say that means they're doing something very right in this space. Now let's scroll down through the various screens, and I'll walk you through how I analyze this valuable data...

The main thing we're looking for on this page is to see how much traffic they're getting. In this case, we see that the site got roughly 490k visits last month (the number that appears will always be for the most recent month). I think we can agree that almost half a million visits in a month is some serious traffic. Now, let's keep going down the page and start breaking things down...

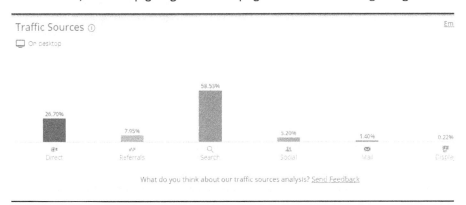

Here, we have the geographic breakdown of the traffic. No surprise, the U.S. comes in at the top. But Turkey being the clear #2? Very interesting indeed. Remember though, this is just the traffic for this particular site — not for the industry.

Pop quiz: what should you be mentally mapping this data back to at this moment? If you said Facebook Audience Insights – and specifically Brazil being #2 – you are correct! There's nothing to do with this fact quite yet, but this is where you'd want your thinking to be right now as we continue.

Note: where it says "See 249 more countries," that link is only clickable if you have the paid version, which is quite expensive. For now, the free version is more than sufficient, as it will give you the top several entries in each category. OK, let's continue...

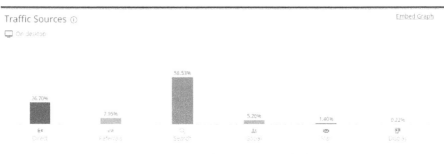

This graph gives you a breakdown of the traffic by source, and indicates that TM.org gets the majority of its traffic through search (around 287k visitors – I get this by multiplying 490,000 visitors by 58.53%). This is useful info at a top glance, but in and of itself is limited. The breakdowns, however, are pure gold. Let's dig in.

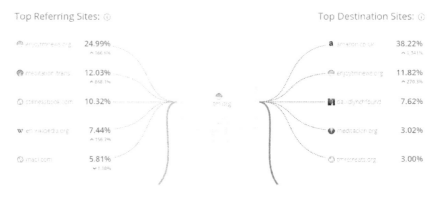

This graphic is fantastically valuable. It is a perfect visual representation of the most common traffic flow to and from the site you're analyzing. The sites on the left are the five most frequent sites people visit before tm.org (i.e. sites that send them traffic), and the sites on the right are the ones they're most likely to go to after. Here are the main points that jump out at me from this analysis:

- Enjoytmnews.org is clearly a key site in this space, as it is the most common site people visit before and after tm.org. Note: next to every site listed here, you can click to open it up. That's what I'd do here, to get an idea of what it's about, and to see what opportunities there may be for siphoning some of their traffic if/when I eventually enter this space. By "siphoning their traffic," I simply mean looking for opportunities to publish content on their site, whether in the form of articles, videos, or ads. When I clicked over to their site, I noticed a link at the bottom called "Share your story." Boom!

- I'd then do similar investigations with the other referring sites on the left side of this graphic (aside from Wikipedia, which is self-explanatory).

- By far the top destination site is UK Amazon. So, I'd want to dig in and see if I could reverse engineer what kinds of Amazon offers they might be making, as it appears to be a key part of their business model.

There's that name David Lynch again. Yet more evidence that he is a major player in this space. At this point, my curiosity would be piqued beyond just making a note of it, and I'd actually Google and see who he is. When I do, I discover that he has a transcendental meditation foundation! Bingo! Identifying key people in a market can be even more valuable than websites. Relationships are everything (And so is spy work! Isn't this fun? Don't you feel like a secret agent, just like I was over two decades ago? Now we can bond over being pseudo James Bonds). ☺

Let's continue down the page and look at tm.org's search data:

43.04% Organic		56.96% Paid	
Top 5 Organic keywords Out of 592: ⓘ		Top 5 Paid keywords Out of 380: ⓘ	
transcendental me...	18.07% ∧ 31.34%	tansiyonu ne düşu...	3.80% ∧ 2,160%
transandantal med...	1.86%	transcendental me...	2.87% ∧ 57.04%
tm	1.36% ∧ 1,896%	disleksi ne demek	0.88%
tm meditation	0.71% ∧ 47.97%	meditasyon	0.88%
trancendental med...	0.47%	konsantrasyon	0.88%

They are clearly active in both organic and paid search. Organic basically means "free." In other words, traditional search engine optimization – trying to get your site ranked high for relevant keywords. Whereas "paid" typically refers to PPC (pay per click) marketing, where you advertise with the major search engines and pay a certain amount per click every time someone clicks on one of your ads for the keywords you're bidding on.

It's hard to overstate how incredibly valuable this information is. To review:

- This is one of the biggest players in the space, and likely a $10-50 million company.
- The left column shows the top keywords they're focusing on ranking for organically.
- The right column shows the top keywords they're actually paying for with their marketing dollars (interesting to note that four of the five are in foreign languages).

This is literally a road map (or should I say, treasure map!) for you to follow, if you enter this space. Why reinvent the wheel when you can see in plain sight what the top players are doing that's working?

Let's keep going...

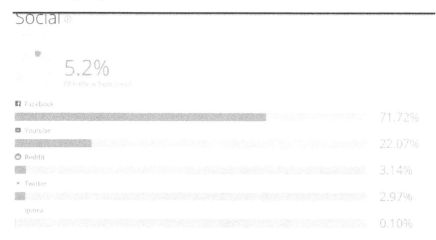

No big surprises here. Facebook and YouTube are where they put most of their social media emphasis. Although it's worth noting that only 5.2% of their traffic comes from social media. I've seen many instances where this number is much higher – sometimes well over 50%. I've also seen cases where a lesser-known social media source delivers a lot of traffic. These are the types of markers you want to look out for.

Moving along...

Display Advertising ⊙

0.22%
Of traffic is from Display Ads

Top Publishers ⓘ

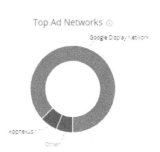

Top Ad Networks ⓘ

Google Display Network

Appnexus

Other

🔵 pictame.com

🔵 definition.org

📷 printanimal.info

The above graphic shows where tm.org is buying its display traffic from. Display advertising simply means ads that appear on websites, and that are not bought from a social media platform such as Facebook. In this case, tm.org gets a very small portion of its traffic (0.22%) from display ads. However, I wouldn't necessarily ignore it, as I find that display traffic can be some of the lowest hanging fruit available. And although tm.org isn't very active in display, you can see exactly where they're buying the little display traffic they do get. The left column, titled "top publishers," shows individual sites where they're likely buying traffic from directly. While the right column – "top ad networks" shows aggregate groups or "networks" of sites they're buying from. The largest display network by far at the time of this book's publication is Google Display Network (GDN). As always, I'll keep these resources up to date for you at www.UltimateVida.com/toolbox.

If you're feeling lost and confused about this whole "buying traffic" or "display advertising" thing, and why that's even an option you'd want to pursue, fear not – I've got some detailed advice coming up for you that's going to blow your mind. Quick spoiler alert: literally every major success I've had online has leveraged the power of paid traffic. So you could say I'm a fan. ☺

But before we go into that, I've got a couple of more goodies for you to finish off our SimilarWeb analysis...

Also visited websites ⓘ   Topics ⓘ

davidlynchfoundation.org
meditation-transcendantale.fr
sfriedman.harvestapp.com
meditation-france.com
meditation.de

world maharishi
film davidlynch lynch
psychology david foundation

On the right is a keyword mind map, which can be useful for reinforcing the main keywords and concepts that are parallel to whichever website and market you may be analyzing (by the way, there's this David Lynch character again!).

On the left, and even more useful in my opinion, are closely related sites that people in this market are also visiting. It will be well worth your while to visit each of these sites and:

- Take the general pulse of the site and its place in the market
- See if there are any opportunities to publish organic (free) content, such as blogs, articles, videos, etc.
- See if there are any advertising opportunities to buy traffic on this site.

Note: You can usually find the answer to b) and c) either at the top or bottom of the page. Look for links such as "company," "about us," "contact" or "advertising."

OK, one final key section of SimilarWeb for us to look at...

Competitors & Similar Sites ⓘ

Boom! I know I must sound like a broken record at this point, but it truly blows my mind that this information is just out there and freely available, if you know where to look (which 99% of people don't, but now YOU do!). ☺ Seriously though, companies spend millions of dollars to compile this sort of competitive analysis, and I'm not exaggerating.

Now, obviously no tool is perfect and this one is no exception. Use your discretion and ignore sites as broad as YouTube and Wikipedia that come up in this analysis. But most of the others? You'll see they're very closely related to the topic at hand, which in this case is transcendental meditation. Again, these could very well be excellent sources of traffic for you down the road – either organic (free), or paid.

And remember the "tree" analogy I shared with you a little while ago, on Facebook Audience Insights? Well, the same concept very much applies here. For example, let's take dhamma.org, which is one of the sites that shows up in the "competitors and similar sites" graphic above. I won't flood you with more screenshots, but guess what happened when I opened it up in a new tab?

First, there was a tab on that site called "courses." Boom! Do you think that might be a good place to eventually list your course? Secondly, I quickly ran this site through the top level of SimilarWeb and found that it got 1.76 Million visits last month! That's over three times the traffic that tm.org (the site we've been analyzing this whole time) gets! Amazing, right?

So that's what I meant by the "tree analogy" applying here. If tm.org is the "trunk," then sites like dhamma.org would most certainly be branches, and then of course there would be branches off of those branches as well. It's not uncommon for one of those "branches" to be even more useful than the original site. Nor is it unusual for a "branch off of a branch" to contain the golden nugget that allows you to break a market wide open. There is truly a stunning amount of opportunity here. You just have to follow the process in this book, keep digging, and have fun with it. ☺

Let's Raise the Stakes and Go "5D"

As potent and powerful as the 3D and 4D elements have been, they've failed to answer perhaps the most crucial question of all: How are these businesses and websites you're analyzing *making their money?*

Sure, you may be able to see some of their product and service offerings here and there. But chances are, you won't be able to see their entire business model just by visiting their site. Most likely you'll only be able to see their "front end" offer, if that.

By "front end," I simply mean their initial or entry level offer – usually for a relatively low price — to "acquire the customer" whom they will then make other offers to down the road. It's actually a good thing that these companies' business models are not so readily obvious – because it gives you the opportunity to go the extra mile by taking a very simple action that almost no one else will take; and in the process you'll gain insights into their business and the marketplace that almost no one else will have!

So how exactly do you get a peek behind the curtain of the key players in your space? It couldn't be simpler – **buy their entry level product and become a customer!** This is one of the best investments and smartest purchases you could ever make. No matter how many "spy tools" you have, you'll still be on the outside looking in to some extent unless you become an actual customer of the company you're analyzing. Once you do, it changes everything. Now you'll get to see their customer care, their upsells, cross-sells, other offers, exclusive invites & invitations for customers only, etc.

Why is this so important? Because this is how the money is really made! It's very unusual for a company to make any serious money with their initial offer. The real wealth and prosperity usually happens on the "back end" in the form of additional, higher-priced offerings to their customers at various points during the customer lifetime span.

In fact, plenty of savvy companies will gladly lose money on the front end in order to acquire the customer. This strategy is known as a "loss leader." The reason they're willing to do this is because they have plenty of offers to make once a customer is in the door, and they know the average conversion rate or "take rate" for each of these offers. This allows them to calculate the "lifetime value of a customer" which in turn allows them to figure out how much they're willing to pay to acquire a customer.

And not to steal the thunder from the upcoming chapter on paid traffic... but know one thing: Whichever company (or individual) can spend the **most** to acquire a customer is almost certainly going to be the leader in any given marketplace.

"Giving Away" Music All the Way to the Bank...

I'll give you an example. I grew up in the 80s and 90s, before the advent and proliferation of iTunes, Spotify, and other digital music platforms. One of the most popular and successful business models in the music space at the time was executed by companies such as Columbia House and BMG Music, who would offer "9 CDs for a penny" or "12 CDs for the price of one." (Yeah, I know I just dated myself with the CD reference) ☺

Obviously, it was impossible for these companies to make a profit on this initial purchase. On the contrary, they'd actually lose money. But the way these offers worked is that once you cashed in that initial offer and became a customer, "all you'd have to do" is purchase three CDs at regular price, for example, over the next year.

Now, once the customer purchased three, the company at least got closer to profitability, as CDs had a very high markup. But here's the real kicker. The way the model worked is that every month, the customer would automatically get shipped the "selection of the month." If they liked it, great — they just pay the regular price (which happened automatically, of course, by the company billing their credit card on file) and keep it. And if not, no problem, they just ship it back and never have to pay.

As you can imagine, if something cool arrives at your door without you having to do anything, there's a chance you might keep it if you like it, even if it's not something you would have otherwise gone out and bought. Also, some people are just lazy and wouldn't go to the trouble of shipping it back, so they'd just keep it and get billed. This is how these companies built their empires, and at Columbia House's peak, it was a **$1.4 Billion** company!

Oh, and in case you're wondering if this model is still alive and well? I'm on a plane right now as I'm writing this chapter, and literally just a few minutes ago in the airline magazine, I saw an extremely similar offer for "Wall Street Wines," where 14 bottles of quality wine plus glasses were offered for only $69.99. Clearly this is another loss leader to enroll customers in their auto-delivery program. Four decades later, and essentially the exact same business model as the BMG Music which I described a moment ago. See what I mean about this stuff being timeless?! You've got the treasure map in your hands. Don't question it or overthink it — just take action!

Action Steps

Check them off - literally, in ink!

List the top 3 sites in your space

Research all 3 in SimilarWeb - and then also research the 2 most relevant further sites for each of them - a total of 9 researched sites

Buy the entry level product for 3 key players in your marketplace

Step 8: Ready, Steady, Go! But Don't Get Caught...

What's going on here?

Now you learn how to DEFEND yourself when other people try to do market research on YOU

From Ghostbusters to the Karate Kid (Unmasking Your Secret Weapon and Bulletproof Vest!)

Remember the iconic movie, "The Karate Kid?" In case you don't (you know, if you were born under a rock ☺), let me refresh your memory...

Do you recall when Mr. Miyagi had Daniel painting his fences, waxing his cars, and doing all sorts of manual labor? At first, Daniel eagerly jumped right in, knowing on some level that he was being taught something, even if he didn't yet know what it was. But he soon grew impatient, wondering what the point of it all was. He finally reached his breaking point and was about to storm out, when suddenly Mr. Miyagi began throwing kicks and punches at him, and to his astonishment, he found himself reflexively using the motions he learned from waxing and painting to defend himself. Daniel's internal light bulb went off, as he realized that by trusting in his mentor and performing the actions given to him, he had unknowingly become **bulletproof**. It was a powerful and pivotal moment for young Daniel.

I realize, Dear Reader-san, that you and I are not face to face (at least not yet). And even if we were, I would never presume to have the infinite wisdom of Mr. Miyagi (and don't worry, I won't throw kicks and punches at you, either). But I suspect that maybe — just maybe — you're channeling our dear friend Daniel-san with the following question:

"If I Can Do it to Them, Can't They Do it to Me?"

Let me address a question and concern that I have a strong suspicion has been running through your mind – at the very least, in the background – during the past few chapters as we've gone into the 3D glasses analysis (yes, I can read your mind, mwah ha ha).

"Well Jesse, it's great that you're showing me all these next-level research and analysis techniques to see exactly what people are doing and how to reverse engineer it. But won't someone be able to do this to me as well? Especially if they get their hands on this book?"

Valid question. And surprisingly, the answer is NO! Provided, of course, that you connect with your tribe in your own unique voice.

Connecting and storytelling makes you bulletproof. Period. Exclamation point! This is the other half of your bulletproof vest! We've already touched on connection, and we're about to go even deeper. And we'll do a powerful deep dive on storytelling as well.

People *might* be able to reverse engineer parts of your business model. But they'll only be able to reverse engineer YOU, if you speak in a generic voice and don't connect with your audience. And let me say that you need absolutely **zero** special skills or talents to connect.

Superman is Embraced for his Kryptonite

Let's take "real and authentic" a step further. The key word we're really looking for here is **vulnerable**. That's right. Don't be afraid to open up and let people in on your fears, doubts, and insecurities. We as human beings are all endlessly flawed and complicated beings. And if you present yourself as anything different, people have a way of sniffing that out.

You may think that people want to follow a superhero. Someone who never gets ruffled or faces adversity. That couldn't be further from the truth. The reality is that people will be watching what you do, and asking themselves if they can do it too. This may not happen on a conscious level – but make no mistake; it's a script that will be running in the back of their minds.

Let Your Tribe See *All* of You... Not Just Your Highlight Reel

Do you think I had fun revealing to you how I sobbed uncontrollably in my filthy shower, as my life fell apart and I had no idea how to put it back together? Of course not. It was incredibly painful to take myself back there and share that with you. But I can't possibly expect you to relate to me, much less follow any advice I give, if you see me as this indestructible, larger than life character. That's just not real. I don't believe I deserve to lead you or guide you if I don't show you all sides of me. I hope that one day I will have the privilege of meeting up with you for a cup of coffee or a glass of wine. And when that happens? You'll see that I'm no more talented or special than you are. You may see my strengths; you may see my flaws. But one thing you'll see for sure is that I'm real.

Presumably, there's someone in your life you'd open up to about the challenging and painful times in your life. Perhaps a family member or close friend? Well, I urge you to do it with your tribe, too. No, you don't have to reveal every last personal and private detail of your life. But let them in on the big stuff. There's really no downside to doing so, and if you don't, they'll sniff it out anyway and you won't seem real to them. And if you do, it will not only make you more relatable to your tribe, but it will feel good, as you'll be speaking and living your truth!

So, between storytelling (which we'll get into very soon) and being vulnerable, believe me when I say that's what makes you bulletproof. Even more so than any particular business model or marketing technique.

And when you combine that with the 3D, 4D and 5D research tools I've just taught you? The extreme depth we went into on audience and market research?

That, my friend, is your bulletproof vest.

Doing this level of research and connecting deeply is your killer app. Others in your space simply won't go as far.

That is what will give you the margin of error to make mistakes and still come out on top.

That is what will allow you to create your Ultimate Vida with*out* being a marketing expert.

That is what will **set you free.**

Bulletproof Weapon #2: Find Your Domino and Knock That @#%& Down!

I want to share with you one of the most powerful studies I've ever seen in my life. It involves dominoes. Yes, dominoes. Twenty-nine of them to be exact.

We've all heard of the "domino effect." But did you know that each domino is capable of knocking down a domino up to 50% larger than itself? In other words, a 2-inch domino can knock down a 3-inch domino, which can in turn knock down a 4 ½ inch domino, and so on. This was proven in a study by University of British Columbia physicist Lorne Whitehead.

Forget two inches though. To really drive this point home, let's be way more conservative and start with the first domino being only five millimeters high. That's less than 1/5 of an inch! In other words, a seriously "micro domino!" Want to know how powerful that micro domino can be, once it gets going in a decisive and purposeful direction? According to University of Toronto professor Stephen Morris, *it would only take 29 progressively larger dominoes for this five-milimeter domino to start a domino effect that would wipe out the Empire State Building*! Say whaaaat?!

I don't know about you, but to me, it's no coincidence that we're talking about exactly 30 dominoes here to have this ultra-powerful effect. What else can you think of that comes in groups of 30 (or 31)? You guessed it – a month! Can you imagine the power that this domino effect can have if executed every day for a month? What about this effect times three, for a quarter, or times 12 for a year? Mind blowing.

Unlocking Your "Big Mo"

The key to creating this domino effect in your life and business – in your new Ultimate Vida – is a very powerful one-word concept that I don't think gets nearly enough attention. I am talking about **momentum**. Sure, we all know what momentum is, but compared to other concepts in the world of business, performance and life in general, our friend momentum tends to fly under the radar.

In a few minutes, we'll make a powerful distinction between strategy and tactics. But for a quick sneak preview, think of the daily execution... as the tactics that will actually knock down the next domino. But of course, if you just line up any random row of dominos and knock them down with no rhyme or reason, you'll just endlessly zig zag and never really get anywhere. So, the strategy side of building this momentum is figuring out exactly what those dominoes should be.

So how do we figure out just what these elusive dominoes are? Well, I've got good news and bad news. The good news is that it's not that hard to figure out. The bad news is that your domino is quite likely something you've been avoiding or that makes you feel uncomfortable. But the best news of all? You don't need to figure out 30 dominoes. You only have to figure out anywhere from one to three – and then knock those same dominoes down day after day.

To explain why I say one to three, I'll give you a peek behind the curtains with a personal example of what my own dominoes are right now. My main domino right now is writing this very book that you now have in your hands! More specifically, I committed to writing a minimum of 1,000 words each and every day with no excuses and no exceptions. If you're thinking that sounds daunting, trust me, I thought that at the beginning, too. In fact, it freaked me out! But I learned two very important lessons along the way, that made this – or any – domino far easier to knock down every day:

When I first decided to write this book, naturally I had to figure out and research what to put in the book. But I also had to learn how to write a book! I had never written a book before, and I wanted to see what wisdom I could glean from the masters! In the midst of my research, I came across a quote from bestselling author Jodi Picoult which quickly became one of my mantras, not only for writing, but for life:

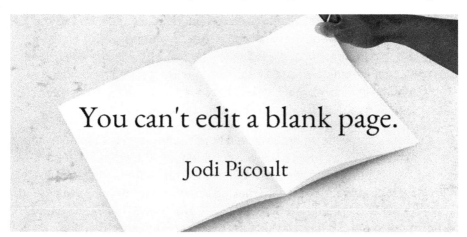

You can't edit a blank page.

Jodi Picoult

This is so brilliant on so many levels. And it applies not only to writing, but to any domino we want to knock down! The takeaway is that we don't have to be perfect. We don't even necessarily have to be good. We can always go back later and make it better. But what we DO have to do is show up and do the daily action that we committed to in order to knock down that domino.

The even cooler lesson I learned is that you can set your daily bar far lower than you may have thought, and still be very successful if you just show up and do it. For example, those 1,000 words a day I committed to? I've found that I can knock them out in an hour or less if I'm inspired and "in the zone." But more importantly, I've found that I can still get them done in under two hours even if I'm not feeling inspired. As the great Stephen King put it, *"Amateurs sit and wait for inspiration, the rest of us just get up and go to work."*

Boom! I can't tell you how true and freeing that quote is. And once again, it applies to any domino we set for ourselves. Put another way, the whole key to knocking down those dominoes is *doing the action you committed to regardless of how you are feeling.* If you think about it, it's very liberating. You're basically giving yourself permission to feel absolutely anything, including sadness, anger, frustration, etc – normal human emotions — but are simply saying that you're going to still do the action while you feel that emotion.

Oh yeah, I mentioned "one to three" dominoes. Well, there were a couple of other areas of my life where I wanted to "up my game" and knock down some dominoes, aside from writing this book. One was my exercise and physical fitness routine. I travel a lot and am not a gym rat, so my mission was to find a workout that I could a) do anywhere at any time, and b) was a low enough bar so I would actually do it. After some research, I ended up with the "Tibetan Rites" (Google it if you want to), with a few tweaks made by a close friend of mine who is a health and wellness guru for additional strength building. This workout takes me around 23 minutes and all I need is a floor with a yoga mat or even just a towel laid across it.

The final area of my life where I wanted to get some serious domino action happening while writing this book was my spiritual, or inner practice. For me (and for right now), that simply means meditating for a minimum of 10 minutes per day. Again, the key to making this work was to not have all kinds of rules of what this meditation is supposed to look like. That would have just stressed me out and defeated the purpose. I won't go talk about what kind of meditation I do, because a) I don't want to distract from the topic at hand, and b) more importantly, there's no right or wrong form of meditation! The key again is to be gentle with yourself. Sometimes those 10 minutes turned into more, and other times they didn't. Either is ok. Sometimes my mind was relatively clear and relaxed, and other times (more often), various thoughts crept in. Again, either is ok. The benefit comes in the daily knocking down of the domino!

Occasionally, I'll get into a good groove and bang out more than 1,000 words, or extend my workout or meditation. You'll find that once you start setting these benchmarks for yourself, you'll start building momentum, and once you do, it will become easier and more natural to "go the extra mile." But even if I just meet my minimums and don't exceed them, it's perfectly OK and I feel like I've "won the day."

Here's the real kicker. All three of these activities combined take me anywhere from an hour and a half to three hours, depending on my level of focus and efficiency. So even in the worst-case scenario of three hours, I still have the majority of the day open for other work and/or personal activities. I'm a big believer that for the majority of us, setting the bar "low" is the way to go, as the more of a cushion we leave ourselves, the more we'll value our time and be able to "relax" into getting our "one thing" done. Now I put "low" in quotation marks because in my opinion, if you correctly identify your one to three things, it's actually not a low bar at all. Because you'll be zeroing right in on the activities that have the highest impact in your life and business.

One final point I will make is to not get in the habit of "banking" extra activity for the following day.

For example, if I write 1,300 words one day, I don't take it to mean that the next day I only have to write 700. Instead, I take the extra 300 as a bonus. The only time that "banking" is acceptable is if you know that for some reason you won't be able to do anything the following day. In these rare cases (and I stress rare, because the idea is to do them no matter what), you would want to knock out double your baseline today. For example, a few days ago, I took a redeye flight from L.A. to Miami, followed by a 3-hour early morning layover, and another flight to Medellin, Colombia. I knew I'd be exhausted and might not be in a state to crank out my 1,000 words. So, I wrote 2,000 the day before. I did, however, meditate on the plane and did my workout in the afternoon when I arrived, rewarding myself with a long, hot shower after. There's always a way!

So, the question now, of course, is how do you find your "Ultimate Vida Domino?" Glad you asked. ☺

The One Thing

In his brilliant book, "The One Thing," Gary Keller says that the best way to identify your "one thing" is to ask what he refers to as the "focusing question," which is:

"What's the ONE Thing I could do, such that by doing it everything else would be easier or unnecessary? Then time block to make it happen. It doesn't have to be any more complicated than that."

Most importantly, he echoes what I said above, which is that if we're being real with ourselves, we just kind of know what our one thing is. In his words:

> *The amazing thing is when people ask themselves the question, they are almost always accurate. People instinctively know what matters most. If you're not sure, look to the people who came before you.*
>
> *Chances are someone has already accomplished what you're trying to achieve and they've shared how they did it (in a book, an article or a blog post). Start with their answers and go from there.*

With that in mind, I've got some awesome news for you. If you have a burning desire to be the architect of your own life... the captain of your own ship... to build your own dream instead of someone else's... to be where you want, when you want, with the income you want... to leave the impact and legacy you want to leave on the world... to create and live your Ultimate Vida... If you say "Hell yes!" to all that? Then I humbly submit to you that this book is your bible, your blueprint, and your treasure map. That this is your "one book" to make it happen (along with ongoing support, of course). The fact that you already have it in your hot little hands gives you an exponential, almost unfair advantage! I can't stress that enough.

With that in mind, let's look at a few different levels of identifying your "one thing" and beginning to chip away at it.

Your Ultimate Vida Domino: Level One

If you currently have a job, chances are your "one thing" (i.e. your main domino) would be to leave that job and create your Ultimate Vida! But, what would that actually look like in terms of a daily activity to prioritize?

Well, that depends largely on the first key decision you'll make: Whether you're going to quit your job NOW and go "all in" on your Ultimate Vida, or whether you want (or need) to start building up some income on the side before you take the leap?

Now, the interesting thing is that the steps you take will pretty much be the same whether you're doing them full time or part time. They'll just happen at different speeds. For example, as I shared with you in my story, I did not leave my job right away – primarily because I had no savings and was not willing to compromise living by the beach in southern California, which is expensive. So, I was militant about going to the library every day during my lunch hour, as well as spending some time in the evenings studying, learning and applying this new craft of internet marketing, which really didn't yet exist in its current form. There was no road map or blueprint to follow whatsoever. I had to create it myself and make it up as I went along. In that sense, you are already way ahead of me, as you have the blueprint and roadmap right here!

So, if you're not willing or able to make the leap right away, ask yourself what daily time frame are you willing to commit to in order to move in that direction?

- Will you wake up an hour earlier?
- Stay up an hour later?
- Cut out some TV, social media, or other activity?
- Use your lunch hour in different ways?

There's no right or wrong answer, really, as long as you carve out a daily block of time and declare it non-negotiable with yourself.

Once you make this decision and declaration? Then you'll be ready to really kick it up a notch and make things happen. I'm excited for you! Let's dive in.

Success in any part of your life can really be boiled down into three steps:

- Have a solid plan and strategy in place.
- Show up every single day and consistently execute it.
- Constantly take in the data and results and be willing to apply it, but do not be quick to jump ship and abandon the strategy.

That's it. Game, set, match. I don't care how many flow charts and Venn diagrams and 57-part sequences and funnels you see. If you've got the three concepts above in place, and they're happening in synergy with each other, you will succeed.

Let's look at each of these three steps.

Step One: Have a Solid Plan and Strategy in Place

Good news – you've already got this one covered! This book is your solid plan and strategy. It's your guide, your blueprint, your treasure map. It's 22 years of living the Ultimate Vida, across many different economic conditions, technology waves, business and marketing trends, and countries & continents; distilled into the pages of this book. And it will be as relevant in one or five or 10 years as it is now, and will therefore remain your roadmap.

Now, I'm not claiming that this book is your only conceivable roadmap. There are plenty of other brilliant books, blogs, podcasts, etc. But I can guarantee you that your first "domino" in this case is to choose ONE guide, path, mentor, etc. If you resonate with this book and with me, I'm thrilled and honored to help you create and sustain your Ultimate Vida. If not, I take no offense, but my advice stands – please find ONE other guide, mentor, etc. that you resonate with, and then stick with the path that he or she recommends.

The only thing I will add is that when it comes to living the Ultimate Vida or anything similar that goes by a different name, I searched high and low for anything even resembling a blueprint and could not find it. And that's why I decided to write this book.

Step Two: Show Up Every Day and Consistently Execute Your Plan

There are no words I or anyone could possibly write that could overstate the profound importance of consistency.

Consistency may not be sexy, but the results and freedom you'll get by being consistent are very sexy indeed.

My second favorite quote of all time (don't worry, I'll share #1 with you when the moment is right ☺) is this:

When nothing seems to help, I go look at a stonecutter hammering away at his rock perhaps a hundred times without as much as a crack showing in it. Yet at the hundred and first blow it will split in two and I know...it was not that blow that did it, but all that had gone before.

Jacob Riis

Boom! This quote still stirs me up every time I read it. You'd be absolutely astounded if you knew how successful you could be by just being consistent. Of the three steps to success I laid out above, step two – consistency – is the one that most often derails people. If you're willing to simply show up every day and knock down your domino no matter what, with no excuses, you'll be shocked to discover what you can accomplish.

Furthermore, consistency will become another go-to weapon in your toolbox that will make you completely bulletproof. Some people may be able to reverse engineer your business model. A small percentage of them may even be able to emulate your strategy (although they'll never be able to emulate your vibe with your tribe). But consistently showing up every single day and smashing your domino? No one, and I mean no one, can knock that off.

A whole new way to look at "POO"

One concept I've been much more mindful of in the past few years that I've seen make a huge difference in my life and results, is "Process Over Outcome." (P.O.O!)

Our greatest sources of angst, stress and worry typically happen when we focus on the outcome. Which is ironic, as the outcome is never in our control. But the process sure as heck is. And wouldn't you know it? When you start focusing less on the outcome and more on the process, a funny thing happens – the outcomes tend to go your way far more often.

So, what exactly do I mean by "process?" Well, if you combine steps one and two above – have a strategy in place and execute it consistently – that can be considered your "process."

"POO," a la Seinfeld?

Perhaps no story illustrates the power of consistency better than the one told by Brad Isaac, who was an aspiring comedian starting out on the circuit.

One serendipitous night, Isaac happened to be in a club where Jerry Seinfeld was performing.

In an interview on Lifehacker, Isaac shared what happened when he caught Seinfeld backstage and asked if he had "any tips for a young comic."

Here's how Isaac described the interaction with Seinfeld...

> He said the way to be a better comic was to create better jokes and the way to create better jokes was to write every day.
>
> He told me to get a big wall calendar that has a whole year on one page and hang it on a prominent wall. The next step was to get a big red magic marker. He said for each day that I do my task of writing, I get to put a big red X over that day.
>
> After a few days you'll have a chain. Just keep at it and the chain will grow longer every day. You'll like seeing that chain, especially when

you get a few weeks under your belt. Your only job is to not break the chain.

Are you beginning to see the immense power of the three-step, big picture strategy laid out in the past few chapters? Let's review:

- Go through the exercises on page 81 to come up with a list of possible markets or niches you can enter.

- Run each of them through the 3D glasses research tools to drill deep into their behaviors, buying habits, and interests, and choose the one that resonates with you the most and that you feel has the greatest chance of success.

- Start building a tribe around this topic and communicate with them in an authentic, vulnerable manner based around storytelling (which we'll cover in the next chapter).

Hear me when I say this: If you follow this formula, stay consistent and don't give up when the going gets tough, you'll literally be able to write your own ticket. Maybe not right away, and almost certainly not without hiccups and challenges. But I truly believe with all my heart – *not to mention from 22 years of applied research and mentoring others* – that this is the most realistic and sustainable path for you to leave your 9 to 5 and create your Ultimate Vida.

Not only is this formula incredibly powerful, but it threads the needle of simultaneously being cutting edge and timeless. It's timeless because this formula worked 100 years ago, and will work 100 years from now. But it's also cutting edge, as you'll be using the most advanced and efficient tools to extract this info, and thanks to www.UltimateVida.com/toolbox, if a better tool becomes available (which will inevitably happen with innovation and evolution), you'll always have it at your fingertips.

Action Steps
Check them off - literally, in ink!

Write down how much time you're goint to spend each day on your jailbreak - be realistic

Write down the path you're going to follow - either UV or an alternative path - but STICK to ONE PATH

Write down the ONE non-negotiable action you will take EVERY DAY

Step 9: Staying in Touch on the Outside

Whether your main way of communicating with your tribe is through email, Facebook groups, forums, Instagram, Twitter, or on a future platform that has not yet emerged... here are the key, timeless principles that you'll want to make the foundation of how you talk to your "peeps."

The Two Es: Engagement & Entertainment!

To Engage, Ask Questions — Don't Lecture

When you start communicating with your tribe, you're almost certainly going to be tempted to teach and educate them. *Caution: this will almost certainly backfire!*

Always remember that your audience will feel more valued and engaged when they are, well... *engaged*! To make engagement happen, you must do everything in your power to make the communication a two-way street.

The best way to do this is by asking questions. But not just any questions. Relevant, timely questions that show you've got your finger on the pulse of their current needs, desires and frustrations.

Most of all, ask *emotional* questions. Questions that make them feel something. Questions that make them want to reply to you on whatever forum the communication is taking place. No matter how good your material is, or how much you may be a natural teacher, no one's really looking to be lectured to.

How do you figure out what questions to ask them? From your 3D Glasses research, of course, which revealed exactly what's important to your audience!

Entertain 'Em! Humor and Suspense Are Your Friends.

You know what people crave, even more than all the brilliant information you have to teach them? They crave laughter, excitement, and entertainment. They crave real human connection.

That's what must be at the heart of each and every communication you have with your tribe. Always imagine your avatar — and whether it's in writing, by video, or any other medium, imagine you're talking to him or her directly. One on one.

Imagine you're at a bar having a drink, shooting the breeze. Sure, you'll probably talk about the topic at hand, because it's an interest and passion that you have in common. But you'll also joke, talk about life, and just hang out. That's the vibe that you want to cultivate.

Remember the hit shows "Friends" and "Seinfeld?" In most episodes, nothing in particular really "happened." It was more about the connection among the characters, and the random, hilarious moments they shared. That's how you want people to feel every time they see you in their inbox or on camera.

Be Consistent to a Fault

If you're gonna come and go, don't even bother. I realize that may sound harsh, but it's the truth, and I'm telling you up front so there are no surprises.

If you want to penetrate people's minds and hearts (and even think about penetrating their wallets at some point), you've gotta become a consistent presence in their lives.

People respond so much more favorably to someone they can count on. Someone who regularly shows up in their lives.

Now before you get overwhelmed, please understand this doesn't have to take more than a few minutes a day. Remember, the idea is to entertain and connect, not give a daily dissertation. You can literally just write them a few sentences or go on camera for one minute. Just don't come and go from their lives and expect to pick right back up where you left off. That's not how it works.

Now I'm not saying consistent communication is the only model that works. I'm saying that if you want to connect at all, make it consistent. Otherwise, just set up some sort of automated system and don't make real-time communication part of your model — but know up front that your connection with your people will not be nearly as strong or deep.

Also — even a simple set of recorded training materials (video or just voice) can create a strangely powerful and REAL connection with your audience — automated or not. The more they hear or see you, the more they feel they know you.

Make no mistake – consistently communicating with your tribe in a heartfelt manner will be another great equalizer and bulletproof mechanism for you. Without it, you can have temporary success. But with it, even when your current strategy, technique or business model dries up (and this *will* happen from time to time), if you've cultivated that relationship with your tribe, you can quickly and easily pivot and they'll likely pivot right along with you because you've earned their trust.

The Mom Test

This is the ultimate gut check. Before you send out any communication, be it written or video, ask yourself "Would I feel good about sending this to my mother?" In other words, are you being clear, human and authentic? Are you putting their needs above your own? And if you make an offer or try to sell something (which is totally fine), would you feel comfortable making that same offer to your mom? Would you feel good about the value she's getting relative to the price she's paying for it?

The Golden Hammer That Makes Your People Fall in Love With You… and Makes You Even *More* Bulletproof

I'm sure you've picked up by now on my not-so-subtle hints that if you can form a solid and genuine bond with your tribe, you'll have a much higher chance of reaching your goals. And we've touched on certain elements of how to form that relationship, such as value bombs, entertainment and humor.

But I'm guessing you might feel somewhat confused or overwhelmed as to how exactly you're going to come up with regular content to send to your tribe.

Well, I've got a three-word solution for you that'll make your life a lot easier, will make them fall in love with you, and should be at the core of everything you do:

Tell. Them. Stories.

Over and over and over again.

If you always remember that your communication with your tribe should be a "Neverending story," you can mess a lot of other things up and be just fine.

That's right – storytelling is your killer app!

Don't worry if you immediately think "But I'm not a storyteller!" — almost everyone feels like that. But you're wrong — because you're human, and all humans tell stories, every single day. You just don't usually notice that's what you're doing.

Seriously, don't worry. It's just a set of simple steps. Here's how you do it.

What do you tell them stories about? Simple – your everyday life! And I don't want to hear that your life is boring or nothing special. Whether you are an international jetsetter or stay home with your kids, trust me, you've got stories to tell. There's never "nothing going on." Here's one easy hack: When you're out and about, waiting in line, or have moments of what you'd consider "down time," instead of scrolling through your phone, just look around you. Observe what's going on and who's doing what, and you'll have constant fodder for stories.

Here's one way you *can* use your phone that'll be a game-changer for you: Start documenting everything that's even remotely interesting, meaningful or funny in the course of your day. Every time something happens that strikes you in some way, either make a note of it on a pad or in your phone, snap a photo of it, or shoot a video of it. Keep all of these seemingly random notes in a "storytelling file" that you can open up whenever you're feeling at a loss for what to say to your tribe. I can't stress enough the importance of recording or documenting what happens to you in some way. Life is so fast-paced these days that if we don't do this, we'll forget the vast majority of what happens.

Next tip: Everything, and I mean everything, can be somehow related back to your central theme or topic that you're communicating to your audience about. Take the transcendental meditation example we've been working with. Literally anything you throw at me, I can somehow work back to meditation. And so can you with your topic. And if you occasionally don't? That's ok, too. There's nothing wrong with sometimes just connecting with them with no particular purpose or motive. Just goes to strengthen the relationship.

Don't Lead Up to the Punch Line... Start With It!

Here's a killer technique that works wonders for me every time I use it: start a story with the most suspenseful, funny or interesting part, even if it took place in the middle or at the end of the story instead of the beginning. Trust me, it works like crazy, and even many extremely advanced marketers aren't doing it. You want to get in on this one!

It will take a while to get used to, as our natural instinct is to start at the beginning. But you want to hook your tribe in right away to what you are saying. Like in the first few seconds. No matter how much they love you, they're busy just like you, and are pulled in a million directions, just like you.

Here's a specific, word for word example of how I used this technique. You're welcome to model it...

_ _ _ _ _ _ _ _ _ _ _ _ _ _ _ _

I had a white-knuckled death grip on my steering wheel as I careened westbound on the 15 freeway in Nevada, totally out of control.

My palpitating heart felt like it was going to leap out of my chest any minute now.

Beads of sweat threatened to pool into my eyes and blind my vision as I came to terms with what I was about to do.

It was one of those stretches of freeway between Vegas and LA with no exit for at least 30 miles, and there was no way in hell I was going to wait that long.

The stakes were way too high.

It was now or never.

Suddenly, instinct took over and I veered off of the freeway from the left lane and did something I never thought I'd do.

*To the astonishment of everyone else on the freeway – and for the first time in my life — **I drove straight across the median.***

I was fully prepared for any one of a million things to go wrong.

Flashing sirens. Getting stuck in a ditch. Or who knows what else.

But somehow, some way, I escaped disaster.

At least for the moment.

And seconds later I was back on the smoothly paved 15, heading east once again.

Back towards the seedy motel about 30 miles outside of Vegas where I had spent the previous night...

But I'm jumping way ahead of myself.

Let me back up a minute and tell you how I got here...

I had just enjoyed an amazing Las Vegas weekend with friends.

But we drove separately because I was heading back to LA and they were continuing on to Arizona.

So I set off midday Monday, fully expecting the usual four-hour drive.

But about 20 miles in, I suddenly found myself completely stopped in traffic. Like the kind where people are getting out of their cars in the middle of the freeway.

So I pulled up Google Maps on my phone to see how long the delay would be and was greeted with the following news:

Time to destination: 4 hours and 9 minutes

With current traffic: 8 hours and 53 minutes

To this day I don't know what caused it. I'm guessing a huge accident. Hopefully nothing catastrophic.

But what I did know is there was no way I was going to spend 9 hours driving.

So I stopped in one of those cheesy looking motels. It was called Buffalo Bill's or Whiskey Pete's or something like that.

You know the ones I'm talking about – that you pass by but never actually think about stopping at.

(FYI, it was actually totally fine. Not much different than staying at a Holiday Inn or whatever.)

The Art of Freedom

Anyway, the next morning after breakfast, I jumped online to check some stats on one of my businesses and do a little writing.

Suddenly I realized it was almost check-out time. But I was in a good groove, so I just wheeled my suitcase down to the lobby and pulled my laptop back out and kept working.

A couple hours later I reached a good stopping point and decided to load up the car and head out.

Only problem, there's one little item I forgot to load up.

MY LAPTOP.

But like an idiot, I didn't realize I had left it behind until I had been driving about 25 miles.

As Ferriss Bueller famously said...

"Here's where Cameron goes berserk."

Only Cameron was me.

Hence my white-knuckled, median-crossing, crazed behavior.

So now I'm heading back at warp speed towards the Buffalo Whiskey Whatever, praying that my laptop is somehow still there and at the same time playing out the devastating "what if" scenarios if it's not.

*Oh, and this is probably where I should tell you that not only is my computer in the laptop bag, but so is some cash and my **passport.***

At the risk of being way too dramatic, let me just say that me without a passport is kind of like a fish without gills.

Traveling is not only a passion of mine, but it's also a lifeline and sanity-bearer at times.

To channel my inner Dos Equis...

"I don't always take off for another country at a moment's notice, but when I do, I prefer to have my passport!"

Yeah.

So here I am trying my best to stay calm and miserably failing, as I pray that my laptop is still there while also praying not to see sirens in my rearview mirror.

Finally I arrive at Buffalo Whiskey Whatever, take the first parking spot I see, spring out of my car and literally start sprinting across the parking lot to more than a few sideways glances.

The rest was a blur.

I ask a security guard if anyone turned in a laptop.

He seems confused and directs me to the front desk.

I wait a few minutes in line behind people checking in to the hotel without a care in the world (if only they knew!).

Finally I get to the front of the line and ask if they have a lost and found.

The burly receptionist with a southern accent asks me what I lost.

I say "My laptop!"

He gives me a once over and speaks in muttered tones into his walkie-talkie and tells me "Wait here, sir" and motions me off to the side.

A couple of minutes later (felt like an hour), he asks a coworker to cover the desk for him and says "Sir, come with me."

He takes me to some back room, opens the door, and before he can even get a word out, I see my laptop bag!!

I yell out "That's it! That's my laptop!" and start walking towards it.

He says "Hold on a minute, sir" and asks me what kind of computer I have, what else is in the bag, etc – rightfully wanting to identify that I'm truly the owner.

I answer his questions and as he's finally satisfied and gets ready to hand me the bag, I say another silent prayer that it's full...

As he hands it to me, I immediately heft it and SCORE!! I can tell by the weight that at a minimum, my laptop is still there!

Le giant sigh of relief.

I then say one final silent prayer and unzip it, steeling myself for what I might find (or NOT find)...and...

YESSSSSSS!!!!!!

My passport and money are right where I left them, and everything is untouched!!

Le joyful gasp of even greater relief.

I am literally so happy at that moment that it crosses my mind to hug Burly Southern Guy.

The Art of Freedom

But instead, I miserably fail in my attempt to play it cool and just keep thanking him as I grin from ear to ear.

As I walk out of Buffalo Whiskey Whatever, I feel like a million bucks. On top of the world. On Cloud 9.

Whatever hyperbole you can think of, I feel it.

Not to mention, my faith in humanity is sky high at that point.

My only regret from this heart-pounding incident?

That I will never know who the pure-hearted soul was who did the right thing and turned in my bag and left it untouched. I will be forever grateful to this decent, kind-hearted man or woman.

Still basking in my relief and gratitude, I (very carefully!) load my laptop bag into the car and set out again for LA.

Happily driving not a mile over the speed limit, I might add.

And no longer caring if it takes me 8 hours and 53 minutes to get back.

(Notice how my perspective on everything is suddenly totally different?)

Then, a half hour or so later, I had an amazing realization...

I was over the moon happy and all I had was exactly what I started the day with!

I didn't jump out of bed that morning and think to myself "Thank God I have my laptop and passport."

No. I just had them. It was a given. It was part of my reality.

But once they were taken away from me and then I got them back, suddenly I was bursting with this newfound joy and gratitude just for getting back what I already had!

So then I started thinking... what if there were some way to exert greater control over my mind so I was in near-constant gratitude?

What if I could have that feeling as a baseline rather than a rare burst of joy when something unexpected happened?

What if it could become my new norm?

How much happier would I be and how much more could I accomplish?

I took a deep dive into this thing called mindset and became rather obsessed.

What I discovered was nothing short of fascinating. Click here to check it out.

I hope you enjoyed my story and I hope it got you thinking! I'd love to hear your insights.

If nothing else, I bet you'll never look at Buffalo Bill's or Whiskey Pete's or those random hotels outside of Vegas the same!

Yours for appreciating the Ultimate Vida,

Jesse

P.S. Tomorrow I'll introduce you to a man I haven't seen in over 20 years, but without him, Ultimate Vida might not exist!

And through that story, you'll immediately discover THE most critical decision you must make to get to where you want to go!

- - - - - - - - - - - - - - - -

That is some serious suspense, if I do say so myself! Right? It's a true story, though. Now, let me say right away before you freak out – no, that's not the kind of story I write every day. Most of the time, it's like 5 or 10% of that.

But you know how occasionally something really amazing or impactful happens in your life? Maybe it's just a few times a year, and if so, that's totally fine. Those are the ones you really want to go deep with, like I did in my example above. Side note: Those are also the ones you might want to turn into blog posts, published articles, viral videos, etc.

Next key point: In case you're wondering how to transition from the suspenseful part of your story and circle back to the beginning, feel free to model my example above. Specifically, this:

"But I'm jumping way ahead of myself. Let me back up a minute and tell you how I got here…"

These words, or words like them, work wonders. Use them. You'll see. ☺

FREE Bonus for Readers of This Book That I Should Probably Charge Hundreds of Dollars For

Would it help you to see my personal "Best of the best" library of my own stories I've used, which you're welcome to model? Including many that are far shorter and sweeter than the one I've just shared above?

I wasn't exaggerating when I said I should (and easily could!) charge several hundred dollars for this. If I did, it would be a bargain! As these stories and others like them have literally been responsible for millions of dollars in sales over the years.

But I made a promise to myself that if I was going to write this book, I would do everything in my power to over deliver and completely blow you away with the value I provide. So, while I don't think it's appropriate to make this book 50 pages longer by inserting a bunch more stories, I also don't think it's appropriate to keep these stories for myself when I could give them to you for you to model.

To get them, just go to www.UltimateVida.com/toolbox. All I ask is that you don't share this URL with anyone who doesn't have this book, as that wouldn't be fair to **you** who took the action to get to this point. Plus, it would just confuse them without having all the context from the book that you've got!

Add Value, but Make it Short and Sweet

Don't get me wrong, when I say to engage them it doesn't mean not to share your knowledge. It just means to share it with short and sweet, value-packed "truth bombs." One of the greatest skills you can develop is the ability to share a valuable lesson in a few short sentences or paragraphs. When you share in this manner, it will make your point stick and be more memorable than when you ramble on and on.

Understanding people's fears, pain points, challenges, and frustrations, on the other hand? This can be learned relatively quickly and easily, and is largely data driven, simply by going through the tools and exercises I've shown you. To say it's powerful doesn't even do it justice. I have seen time and time again how "average marketing" can be very successful with the right audience and a deep understanding of who they are as people. While, conversely, pro-level marketing without nailing down the audience and a deep understanding of them can result in a spectacular flop.

Action Steps
Check them off - literally, in ink!

Write an emotional question for your audience

Choose how you're going to record your daily moments of content

Write the first line of the most dramatic story from your life about your topic

Step 10: You've Done It — Now How Do You Stay Free?

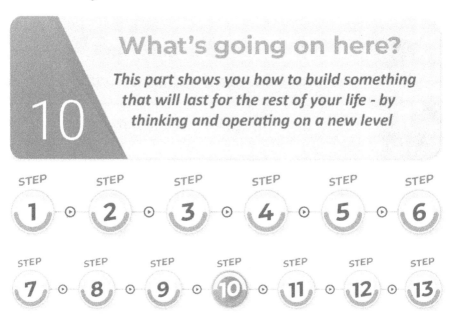

The above chart was posted on ResearchGate.net and is brilliant. It's also super important to understand in order to not only make the leap to your

Ultimate Vida, but to be able to sustain it once you do.

Neither strategy nor tactics are more important than the other. They are both crucial. Another way to break it down and frame this chart is that strategy is the plan, while tactics are the execution. If you have a good plan with poor execution, chances are you won't succeed. And neither are you likely to succeed if you skillfully execute the wrong strategic plan.

S Before T...

Here is the real key: the strategy drives the tactics. Always remember this! S comes right before T in the alphabet, and so it is with strategy and tactics. This does NOT mean that strategy is more important. It simply means that strategy is the driver.

If you follow both the strategies and tactics laid out in this book, and keep moving forward and don't give up, you'll have an excellent chance of escaping your day job and creating your own version of your Ultimate Vida! Very exciting, right?!

But what happens in three years or five years or 10 years from now... or heck, maybe even six months from now (an Internet year is like a dog year!) when the same tactics are less effective or maybe even non-existent?

The reason I have been able to sustain the Ultimate Vida for two decades now, while countless others have come and gone, is not because I am smarter or more special than they are. It's because I've adhered to timeless strategies that will work in any economy, any political climate, and any phase of business or technology. And I have then applied the most effective current tactics and platforms to these strategies, pivoting or updating them when necessary.

For example, one strategy that's critical to your success and gets a lot of focus in this book is gaining a deep understanding of your audience so that you can connect with them.

To properly execute this strategy, I gave you a number of tactics that we referred to as the "3D Glasses tools." Take comfort in knowing that the strategy and its importance will never change. Since the beginning of business, those who've understood and connected best with their audience have had the most success. That will be just as true 10 or 100 years from now as it is today – regardless of what the latest and greatest tools and platforms are. But those tools and platforms are important – critically so. Which is why I've emphasized the link www.UltimateVida.com/toolbox throughout this book, and will always keep it updated for you.

The last line on the chart above illustrates this point brilliantly with just a few words:

Strategic = long time frame; tactical = short time frame.

In other words, the strategy defines the overarching moves you want to make for your business and your life. The tactics represent the specific actions to take in the short term to execute those moves. So, the tactics can change, but the strategies remain constant. The strategy is your marathon, while the tactics are your sprint. You need both to win the race!

The other line on the chart that I want to highlight is "Difficult to copy" vs. "Easy to copy." This is the most important factor of all in my opinion. Remember earlier, I was talking about making yourself "bulletproof" by connecting deeply with your audience? That's a great example, because connecting with your audience is a strategy, not a tactic.

Let me once again call out an uncomfortable truth that I alluded to before; one that I'm sure you've already thought of.

All of those competitive research tools I showed you? The 3D and 4D stuff? In a sense, they are double-edged swords. I'm sure it crossed your mind that if you are able to find all this info about other businesses and websites and their audiences, then it stands to reason that others will eventually be able to look at what you're doing as well.

Yeah, not so much. You're good. And here are the key reasons why:

- The amount of people who are both aware of the tools I've shared with you in this book and actually know how to use them is miniscule. I'm talking far less than 1%. So, I wouldn't worry too much. You've got a serious treasure map in your hands!

- If you connect with your audience in the manner we've talked about and truly form a bond with them, forget about it. People can "reverse engineer" you until the cows come home, but they still won't be able to replicate your success!

• No quantity of data points will enable someone able to fully suss out your strategic positioning, and why you do what you do. It's just not possible.

So, as long as you have a strategic focus – an overarching rhyme and reason to what you do – I will double down on my earlier claim that you can and will become "bulletproof" no matter how many "spy tools" are available.

Summarizing Strategy vs. Tactics

If I had to sum up this whole strategy vs. tactics business in just one sentence? It would go like this:

Strategy is determining *what to do*, tactics are determining the actions to *get it done*.

Put another way, strategy is about winning the game before it even begins, while tactics are about proper execution once the game begins to ensure that it is indeed won.

How does that relate to this book you've got in your hands?

Strategy: Leave your job and build an online tribe

Tactics: Choose a market, validate its potential, demonstrate value, create connectivity and belonging, etc (the steps that this book lays out)

I am pleased to say that this book contains your **entire** strategy.

It also contains a **complete tactical blueprint** for how to execute on your strategy and turn it into reality. I am extremely confident that if you put your blinders on, execute on everything in this book and don't give up, you *will* achieve your goal.

As I've promised several times, the strategies in this book are completely timeless and will not change — and I highly recommend that you don't divert from them.

What the book does not — and can not — account for are potential changes to the tactics, vis-a-vis which tools, platforms, websites, etc. will be most useful to execute the tactics as time passes. The book also does not go into exhaustive depth on every single tactic; if it did, it would be well over 1,000 pages!

But fear not, I've got you covered at www.UltimateVida.com/toolbox with the best tools kept fresh and updated, *and* resources to get into even greater depth on the tactics!

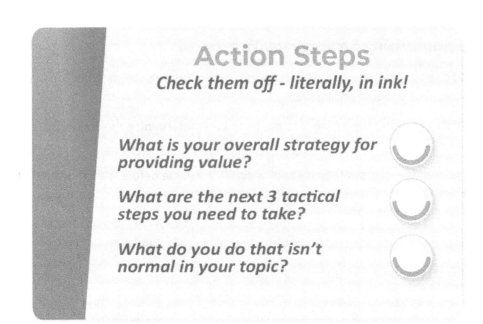

Action Steps
Check them off - literally, in ink!

What is your overall strategy for providing value?

What are the next 3 tactical steps you need to take?

What do you do that isn't normal in your topic?

Step 11: Putting Cash in the Bank (Not Robbing It)

Building Emotional Capital With Your Tribe Earns You the Right to Unlock its *Financial* Capital

I'm sure you've noticed the multiple times I've stressed to you to not focus (yet) on what kind of business you'll have, or what products and services you may sell. I've said over and over again, but it still bears repeating, that by FAR the most important thing you have to nail to be successful is to answer the question "Who you gonna serve?" and then actually serve 'em! And by "serve," I mean form a genuine relationship with your audience and communicate with them consistently on a personal, heartfelt level. If you do that? And I mean **truly** do it? You'll soon discover that you can be successful beyond your wildest dreams with almost *any* business model.

Put another way, you'll be earning **unseen money** (that you'll soon be able to cash in!) right from day one with each and every message you send to your tribe. With each and every act of service or act of love. With each and every connection. With each and every engagement or entertainment piece you send or post!

If you follow this process, and give selflessly and genuinely? You'll find that an interesting thing happens along the way. There will come a time when your tribe will completely let their guard down, because you've proven to them that you truly care and have their back. Once this happens? Not only will they be willing to spend money with you, but they'll actually be *eager* to. You'll notice your tribe more receptive to your communications. Responding and engaging with you with more frequency and emotion. Perhaps engaging with each other as well. Quite possibly alerting others to your messages and/or offers.

Once this time comes, it'll be finally time to start "testing the waters," so to speak, with more systematic strategies, tactics and offers. Aren't you excited? ☺

Let's look at a step-by-step breakdown of the exact actions to take at this stage for maximum results...

Step 1: Identify Their Burning Problem and Give Them a Result That Solves It

Your 3D glasses research (particularly forums in this case) should have uncovered the main challenges, frustrations and pain points that your audience is facing. At this point, your only job is to call out that problem, and present a solution.

Key point: one problem, one solution. Do NOT try to solve multiple problems at once here. You will only confuse and overwhelm the people you want to help. Don't worry if you're unsure if you've selected the "perfect" problem. Just start with the one that seems to be the most pressing. If it turns out to not be the most burning one, your audience will tell you, and you can always pivot. In fact, if you truly don't know what their main problems are (although you should if you've done your research!), then just ask them. That's why establishing the relationship is the real key above all – because they will simply tell you what they want. And this is worth its weight in gold, as you'll soon be able to monetize it.

Let's take the weight-loss space to illustrate the point. An example of the "one problem, one solution" framework here would be "Lose 10 pounds." It would NOT be "get slimmer," "be more healthy," or anything vague and abstract of that nature. The "problem" here is the extra 10 pounds that people want to lose. The solution? This is where you swoop in and give them a step-by-step path to follow. "Do X, Y and Z and you will lose 10 pounds." And then, of course, detail exactly what X, Y and Z are.

"OK Jesse, but how do I "ask my audience" when there is no audience yet?! How do I start talking to my audience?" Glad you asked. ☺

There are a few different ways you can do this:

- Do you know of anyone in your life (friends, family, colleagues, etc.) who is facing the problem that you can help solve? If so, jump right in and help them solve it! For free. Yes, I said free. It's going to be very difficult to eventually sell something if you're not able to show proven results. It's also a great litmus test to make sure you can deliver the desired solution before you start spending time and money to promote this business. Don't worry, plenty of multi-million-dollar businesses started by working for free and demonstrating results.

- If you don't have any personal contacts you can help, fear not – there are other options for finding and reaching your "peeps"...

  o You could start a forum similar to the meditation one I showed above. Forums have been around for over 20 years, and they're not going anywhere. Just google "free forum software" and you'll find various options. Which platform you use is NOT the chief concern right now. You can always build a more robust version later. Right now, you just want to find and connect with your audience.

Right now, Facebook groups are all the rage and the cool thing about this is that Facebook does a lot of the heavy lifting FOR you in terms of finding your ideal members. I've got a great resource for you on building a Facebook group at www.UltimateVida.com/toolbox. As always, if something better becomes available, I'll update it for you.

If you don't want to start a group or forum and have to post all the time, you could just put up a simple one page "site." I say "site" because you really don't even need a full website at this point. You just need one page – most commonly called a "landing page" – that asks people what their most pressing challenge or frustration is when it comes to your topic, and then collects their email address. Once you have their email, you can send them automated messages as well as personal ones, where you start a dialogue, invite them to have a conversation, etc. Oh, and if you are thinking to yourself "That's great, but how do I get traffic to that page?" (Yes, I can still read your mind, mwah ha ha). There are numerous ways, and I've got a whole section for you on traffic coming up, but it mostly boils down to:

- You can get "free" traffic (also known as "organic") through posting in forums, blog articles, social media, etc.), search engines, writing your own articles, recording videos and sharing your link on YouTube, Facebook, etc.

- Or you can run paid traffic (aka ads) through Facebook, Google, or industry specific sites. Surprising as it may seem, I actually FAR prefer paid traffic to free, and I'll tell you why two chapters from now. ☺

Crucial point about all of the above: Do NOT get overwhelmed or intimidated by the technical side of things! I cannot stress that enough. If you do, it will paralyze you, and you'll never get anywhere.

I know you might be thinking "That's easier said than done – I have no idea how to do ANY of this stuff." Well, for what it's worth, I'm probably the least technical guy you'll ever meet. It's funny; people I meet always assume I must be technical because I've had so many online businesses. Nothing could be further from the truth. My family and friends know I'm not technical, of course, and they find this perception of me hilarious.

The real money is in understanding who to reach and how to help them solve their problems (i.e. the stuff you've been reading about in this book). I literally cannot not write a single line of code to save my life. Nor have I ever built a web page – except using point and click tools and software! And back in the day, these tools weren't 1% as robust as they are now. My favorite ones that you can start using right away – even if you've never done business online or had a website before – can be found at www.UltimateVida.com/toolbox. And as always, I will keep this page updated for you should better ones become available!

I want to take this rant even a step further, because it's that important. When I take on new students and clients, their questions often go something like "Should I use AWeber or Mailchimp? (two email/autoresponder providers). Or "Which is better, Clickfunnels or Leadpages?" (two point and drag web page and marketing funnel builders).

My answer is almost always "They're both good, but that is far from your most pressing question right now." There have been many multi-million dollar businesses built on all four platforms I just mentioned, as well as dozens of others!

Once you make your first million, then by all means get really granular about the finer points of each program and how it might slightly improve your results. But until then, I implore you to just pick ANY of the tools at www. UltimateVida.com/toolbox. I have vetted them ALL for you, and each one will serve you very well. So just pick one in each category as needed, and then focus all of your time and energy on following the strategies and tactics laid out in this book! You will thank me later. ☺

Step 2: Deliver the Result That Solves Their Burning Problem

Once you're clear on what their burning problem is, the next step is to solve it for them.

Those four words bear repeating: **solve it for them**.

The key point here is that you are NOT going to *tell them how to solve it* – you're actually going to solve it for them (i.e. tell them what the solution is, or better yet, deliver the result they desire).

Now before you get intimidated or think that you're going to spend all your time solving people's problems, relax. **You're only going to do this 10 times.** That's right, you're going to select 10 people in your audience or tribe or market or whatever you want to call it, and you're going to spoon-feed and hand-deliver them the solution to their problem.

Trust me on this one, and stay with me. Remember the Mr. Miyagi lessons. It will soon become clear why it's so crucial to do this 10 times, and why doing it 10 times will be your key to transforming thousands of lives and setting yourself free.

But before we go there, I want to stress the importance of over-delivering and wowing people here. You want to completely knock these 10 people's socks off with the solutions and results you provide. I'm serious – no stopping until 20 socks are on the floor.

It doesn't matter how you deliver the solution. It can be in writing, on a phone call, a video chat, a face-to-face meeting, however you choose. Feel free to play to your strengths here. But really go all out.

You only have one very simple goal with these 10 people. In fact, it's so simple that it can be put into one single word:

T-R-A-N-S-F-O-R-M-A-T-I-O-N

The story (and reality!) needs to go like this: before connecting with you, they were lost, confused or frustrated about how to achieve the result they desired. They felt like they didn't know where to begin. They were almost ready to give up. Then you came along, lifted the fog from their eyes, and presented them with a burst of clarity that they'd never had before. You not only hand-delivered this result to them, but you delivered them the keys to the kingdom – showing them how they could continue to achieve this result repeatedly in their lives whenever they want to, by simply following the steps you laid out for them.

Step 3: While You're Delivering the Result That Solves Their Burning Problem, Document Everything You Do

Here's what's probably happening for you right now. You're moaning and groaning as you read that you're supposed to document everything you do for these 10 people. You're thinking that takes the fun away and makes the whole thing more boring and tedious. You're thinking you can just do what you do by instinct, on autopilot. Who needs documenting?

Well, it's time to flip that script and get you more excited about documenting your process than you ever thought possible.

Why?

Because documenting will set you free.

Let me say that again: *documenting will set you free*.

I spent many years not documenting, and it's cost me hundreds of thousands – if not millions – of dollars.

Yeah. Painful.

So, learn from my costly mistake, and don't be me.

You probably see where I'm going with this, but in case the dots aren't connecting, let me give you a Miyagi-style sneak preview...

- Showing them how to solve their one most burning problem will probably be worth between $29 and $99 a pop to you – and there is no limit to the amount of volume you can do

- Showing them how to take that one burning problem and solve a bigger, related issue in life as part of a larger framework will likely be worth between $100 and $1,000 a pop to you – again, with no limits on volume

- Actually solving their problem with them or for them? Could easily be worth anywhere from $1,000 to $10,000 and up. This time, volume is not unlimited as your time will be involved, but at that price point, you do a couple of those a month or even a few per year, you're in pretty good shape — and if you've documented well enough, that will give you a vital headstart if you decide to start training other people to do this on your behalf and create a nice passive income stream for yourself ☺

The entire key to eventually being able to monetize at these three levels is documenting the process by which you solve people's problems. As once you do, you can turn it into:

- Reports
- Diagrams
- Flow charts
- Audio
- Video
- Or whatever your preferred method of dissemination

And this material can then be turned into:

- Ebooks
- Courses
- Seminars
- Coaching
- Services rendered
- Or any other way you wish to package it

The Timeless "First Touch" Approach to Connecting With and Monetizing Your Tribe

Remember how I promised you that everything in this book will be timeless? So, check this out. In 1999, I wrote an article where I coined the term "MDA" (Most Desired Action), which ended up being a big hit. My argument in the article was essentially that far too many websites were nothing more than electronic brochures, with way too many links and options. Which is fine for huge corporations more concerned with branding. But for the rest of us who are interested in eliciting a response from the consumer (i.e. direct response marketing), we need to have ONE most desired action on each web page that we want people to take. And we want to focus all text, images, links, videos, etc. on people taking that one action. This idea is also sometimes referred to as "CTA" (call to action).

So, how's this for putting my money where my mouth is, when it comes to timeless concepts? Here we are in 2020; 21 years after I wrote that article, and focusing on the MDA is *still* my most recommended method for connecting with and building your tribe.

Is that because I haven't tested or experimented with other approaches? Quite the contrary. I am pretty much the ultimate lab rat when it comes to online marketing, and have tested just about everything under the sun.

But, I freely admit that I have a bias towards "evergreen" strategies that are going to work month after month, year after year. This approach is much more conducive to the freedom lifestyle than constantly being on the treadmill and emotional roller coaster of trying every new trick and gimmick in the hope that you hit a home run. The reason why I keep coming back to this approach is quite simply because it works, and always will.

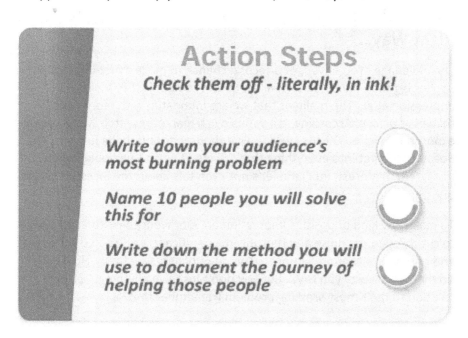

Action Steps
Check them off - literally, in ink!

Write down your audience's most burning problem

Name 10 people you will solve this for

Write down the method you will use to document the journey of helping those people

Step 12: The Map That Will Take You to Safety

How to Pierce Through the Noise and Touch Them the Right Way...

The old adage "You never get a second chance to make a first impression" applies big time online. First of all, you have to fight just to make any impression at all. The reality is that we are inundated with more "info" than ever before. According to a Yankelovich market research study, we are exposed to over 5,000 ads per day. Five thousand! And that's just ads. That doesn't even get into everything that's flying at us on Facebook, Twitter, Instagram, Pinterest, etc. (and let's not even talk about the incessant pings on our smartphones...).

To make any kind of positive impression on your website visitors, you've got to cut through the noise and rhetoric in a significant way. You've got to grab and grip their attention. Almost to the point of shocking them. How do you do that? In a word, you GIVE. But you don't just give anything. You give a solution to their most pressing problem (remember that?).

So, you want your "first touch" with your tribe to have a distinct vibe of giving. The mechanism we use to achieve this is called a **"landing page."** This page is just what it sounds like – a page that people land on with one specific purpose or MDA (most desired action) – not to be confused with your entire website with a variety of links. I'll show you a few different models you can use here, based around a promo I did recently where I offered people a report titled "The 5M Formula for the Ultimate Freedom Lifestyle."

Model Number One: The Classic Opt-In Landing Page

Also known as a "squeeze page" or an "opt-in page," this is typically a very short web page with a headline and a call to action, referencing something of value that you will give people in exchange for their email address. Here are a couple of variations that I've used:

This follows a classic formula of laying out a specific aspirational benefit in the headline (traveling the world and creating a lifestyle you love), followed by a sub-head which says what they'll get and what it is, followed by a space for them to enter their email. It's also accompanied by a lifestyle image of me in San Sebastian, Spain that supports the text and offer on the page.

Here's another variation:

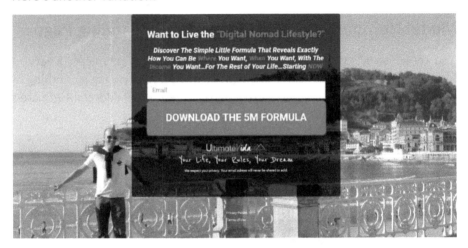

This variation is very similar, but specifically targets digital nomads, so I changed up the text a bit. Notice that the image is the same. Whenever testing a new version against your existing winner or "control" (i.e. "split testing" or "A/B testing"), you want to make sure to only change one variable. Otherwise, it will not be a valid test. For example, same text with two different images, or same image with different copy (text).

In the next chapter, we'll get into some specific split test examples that'll blow your mind (and your bank account, if you implement them)!

Here's another variation that uses a slightly different technique:

Ultimate*Vida* /\/\

Your new life of absolute freedom starts right now and it's called the **Ultimate Vida.**

It's both an art and a science; magical yet methodical.

The Ultimate Vida is both the journey and the destination from which greater journeys begin.

It's your platform to shine your brightest light, to give the world your best and highest self. In our Ultimate Vida, we live in gratitude, think big and have fun!

We travel often and our lives are forever enriched by doing so.

We learn languages and broaden our horizons.

We build wealth, give generously and receive abundantly.

We find strength in our vulnerability. We love passionately, laugh heartily and create breathtaking memories.

We are a worldwide tribe of **brothers and sisters**

who always have each other's back.

The Ultimate Vida is your life's work and legacy.

Your masterpiece - your magnum opus.

Ultimate Vida – Your Life, Your Rules, Your *dream.*

Do You Want This Life For Yourself? Discover the Surprising "5M" Formula That Shows You Exactly How To Get It...

Email

DOWNLOAD THE 5M FORMULA

In this variation, instead of using the classic headline, sub-head approach, I actually just lay out the Ultimate Vida Manifesto and then basically say "Hey, want this kind of lifestyle? If so, just give me your email and I'll show you how."

The idea of a Manifesto is to inspire people and make them viscerally feel like this is something they want to be a part of. Another goal of a Manifesto is to lead people to a clear yes or a clear no. I think you'd agree that after reading something like the Manifesto above, it would be pretty hard to be on the fence. Chances are, you're either a "hell yes" or a "not for me." Although, given that you're reading this book, it's pretty much a given that you're a "hell yes." But I digress... ☺

Now, let's look at a completely different technique:

Could A Four Word Parisian Phrase First Uttered 346 Years Ago Hold The Key To *Finally* Unlocking Your Ultimate FREEDOM Lifestyle?

Imagine yourself in 17th century Paris... 1671 to be exact.

Dressed to the nines in your best petticoat breeches with ruby-red ruffles, you venture out to the Mouton Blanc cabaret on rue du Vieux-Colombier for a night out on the town...

Three of the greatest writers and artists of the time – *Jean de la Fontaine, Molier and Jean Racine* – are sitting at the corner table sipping champagne from *Monsieur Dom Perignon* himself (before he had his label!) and exploring the great ideas and philosophies of the day.

You try not to stare, but you can't help but be mesmerized by these gentlemen.

There is just something about them. They ooze *power, charisma, freedom and possibility.*

At the next table over?

Is the neo-classical critic and essayist Dominique Bouhours.

Like you, Monsiuer Bouhours notices these men. And like you, he is riveted. And he then utters for the first time a magical 4 word phrase which would forever capture our imagination and to this day represents how we all want to be and feel...

In this variation, rather than using the classic "squeeze page" approach, I instead opt for storytelling (remember how important that is?). The idea here is to really engage people in a story and intrigue them. I have pasted in about 1/3 of the story, and they read the rest by scrolling down, and then I reference the 5M Formula and ask for their email at the bottom of the page.

"OK, But How the Heck Do I Make a Landing Page?!"

The quick answer that'll hopefully ease your mind?

You don't have to do it yourself, nor do you have to spend a lot of money.

Let me briefly elaborate...

Landing Page Option #1

One resource I've had a lot of success with over the years is Fiverr –
www.ultimatevida.com/fiverr.

Fiverr is an online marketplace where you can hire out just about any
service you can think of for your business. It started in 2010 and as the name
suggests, was originally a marketplace where most services cost only $5.

To this day, you can still hire out quality jobs for as little as $5. In fact, the
Ultimate Vida Manifesto I just shared with you? It would have cost me only
$5, but I paid $15 for rush delivery – still quite a bargain!

To use Fiverr to find a landing page designer, I'd type terms such as "landing
page," "squeeze page" or "opt-in page" into the search box. Then, you can
review the providers by price as well as their rating and feedback from other
users.

One clever little bonus technique I've used over the years is to hire multiple
people on Fiverr to do the same job, pick the one I like best, and in many
cases, that provider ends up being part of my ongoing team! This will depend
on your budget, of course, but with the low prices that most Fiverr providers
offer, it can be very doable.

Landing Page Option #2

If you're more the "do it yourself" type, and don't want to depend on
and wait for others to build you pages, I'd recommend signing up for a
ClickFunnels account at www.ultimatevida.com/clickfunnels.

ClickFunnels is definitely more expensive than Fiverr would be to get an
individual landing page built. However, if you want to be able to create
multiple, or even unlimited pages – or be able to take immediate action on
an idea you have without waiting for anyone, ClickFunnels is what I'd go with.
And if you're going to make landing pages a central part of your ongoing

operation – which I'd strongly recommend – then ClickFunnels will actually end up being cheaper than Fiverr.

Landing Page Option #3

If you're further along in the process and are considering having a full web site built (or already have one), I'd suggest going with WordPress – www.ultimatevida.com/wordpress.

WordPress is the most versatile and mainstream website and content delivery platform available at the time of this writing. It's not quite as "point and click simple" as ClickFunnels, but it's still quite doable as a "do-it-yourself" platform if you want to go that route. And it's also extremely universal, meaning that if you decide to contract out the work instead, you can easily do so, as almost all designers can work with Wordpress.

How to Make the Decision

- If you don't want to mess with tech stuff and would rather pay someone else a very reasonable price to bring your ideas to life, go with Fiverr

- If you are the "do-it-yourself" type, and/or want to be able to execute on your ideas at a moment's notice without having to be a techie, ClickFunnels is your answer

- If you already have a bigger vision for your site/tribe/platform and want to build out an entire website around it, Wordpress is your best bet

- Most importantly, know that you can't go wrong. Whichever of these three paths you choose to start with, you can always shift gears as your business evolves or if you want to go in another direction.

Action Steps
Check them off - literally, in ink!

Choose your landing page provider

Choose where you're going to get a landing page designed

Get your first landing page designed

Step 13: Buying Off the Cops—You'll Never Get Arrested Again

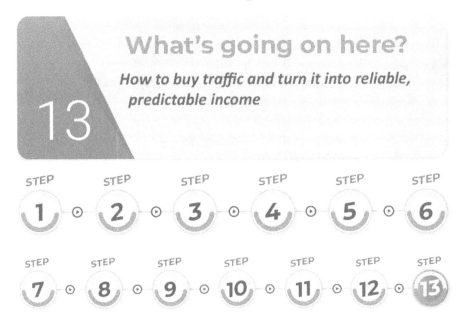

We've spent a great deal of time and energy in this book establishing how and why understanding your tribe on an intimate level and connecting with them is the great equalizer. Focus on that, and you can:

- Make yourself bulletproof
- NOT have to be an expert marketer or businessman/woman
- Pretty much write your own ticket

But here's the rub with building a tribe organically (meaning through hustle, PR, and other free or "guerilla" methods): It can be painfully slow, really test your patience, and take quite some time before you build a large enough tribe with the requisite trust factor so that you can begin monetizing.

So, I'm going to come right out and make a bold suggestion that will NOT be popular or win me many friends, but in my view is also what will set you free and get you to the lifestyle you seek.

I recommend that you focus on PAID traffic.

That's right. I am telling you to voluntarily PAY for your traffic rather than try to get it for free.

Now, before you think I've gone stark raving mad, here are three very powerful reasons I'm advising you to take this approach:

- With paid traffic, you acquire data exponentially faster than with free traffic – and data trumps absolutely *everything* when it comes to decision making.

- Paid traffic is infinitely more scalable and controllable than free traffic. If you figure out how to make $1.50 or $2 for every $1 you spend, chances are you can scale that up hundreds if not thousands of times.

- Time is money and paid traffic is massively more conducive to automation and freeing up your time than hustling for free traffic.

Let's look a bit deeper into each of these three points, and make them fun. ☺

How and Why to Turn Yourself Into a Data Bounty Hunter

Remember how many times I've hammered away at the idea that building a tribe and earning their trust is the great equalizer? And that if you do it properly, you can write your own ticket, whether you're a business and marketing expert or not?

Well, the same is true with data acquisition!

Why?

Because the most dangerous kryptonite that can sabotage our effort is **opinions** – and not just others' opinions, but also *our own*.

But hear this now, and take it to heart: even the most educated and qualified opinions cannot match the indisputable facts that data provides!

Let's drill down on the word "data," as it's way too boring and blah blah, right?

When most people think of data, they think of data entry, IT, or other technical mumbo jumbo. Booooring!

But make no mistake: Data ROCKS. Data is exciting. And most of all? Data

The Art of Freedom

can literally set you FREE!

How?

Glad you asked ☺

I never lose.
I either win
or learn.

Nelson Mandela

Remember all the lessons earlier in this book about researching your audience, putting on your 3D glasses, and connecting intimately with your tribe?

Well, if you follow those steps, you'll be WAY ahead of the game and be well positioned to build an epic business and lifestyle.

But here's the thing...

As powerful as all that research is?

And as much as it reveals...

It still can't hold a candle to putting an actual offer in front of people and seeing how they respond.

Now, relax... by "offer," I don't mean you have to be selling something. It could just be asking them to sign up for a free report, etc.

And guess what?

Their response (or lack thereof) is DATA!

Once you've identified who your tribe is, and started connecting with them, you'll need to find out which...

- Text
- Images
- Videos
- Designs
- Calls to action
- Offers
- Colors
- Etc.

...they respond to most favorably!

You'll also want to discover which...

- Gender
- Age group
- Location(s)
- Income level
- Family/relationship status
- Device (desktop, mobile, etc)
- Time of day or night
- Etc

...responds best to your messaging.

This process is FUN and fascinating!

If you only remember one thing, remember this: Data trumps opinion – Every. Single. Time!

Now, I consider myself a fairly savvy marketer. But, I must admit, every time I run a test, something about the results surprises me! It doesn't matter how much I think, assume, or even "know" people will respond a certain way. Inevitably, the data paints a slightly (or vastly!) different picture!

So, if this isn't proof that gathering data is the great equalizer, I don't know what is.

And what's even better?

It's astonishing how tiny a percentage of people building something online are actually data driven. Most of them just go by their own assumptions, fly by the seat of their pants, and take their best guess at what will work or not work.

You'll be playing chess while they're playing checkers, always a couple of moves ahead – simply by seeing how people respond, tracking it, and adjusting accordingly!

How Testing Will Crack the Code and *Set You Free*

Want to see some mind-blowing examples of how powerful this data gathering thing can be? And how much difference it can make in your response rate, and ultimately your bank account?

Remember in the last chapter, I showed you how to use landing pages to grab people's attention, make a good first impression, and enroll them into your tribe? Let's drill down further and look at how testing different versions of landing pages can dramatically impact response rate.

Landing Page Example #1: 102.5% Increase in Response for Groove CRM Software

ORIGINAL DESIGN

PERSON DESIGN

102.5% ⬆

Remember in the last chapter with my own Ultimate Vida landing pages, I had a few different concepts? There was the classic squeeze page, the version with the Manifesto, and the longer-form, storytelling page.

This is the same phase Groove was in — testing completely different concepts. In this case, their theory is that the image of the woman in the second version is responsible for the dramatic increase. They may well be right, but the truth is, there's no way to know because multiple variables were changed.

The process here is to start with several versions that are completely different from one another, and once you determine which is the winner, start getting more granular and testing one variable only. Like this...

Landing Page Example #2: A Danish Company Boosts Response by 38.26% Just by Changing One Word!

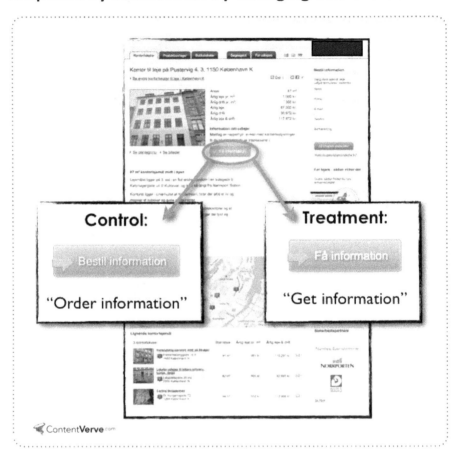

In this example, literally everything about the two versions is exactly the same, except that the version saying "Get information" yields a 38.26% higher response than the version saying "Order information." Can you believe there's such a vast difference in response just by changing one word?!

My theory here is that "get information" is more user-friendly and it may have been premature to talk about placing an order. But the bigger point is that theory and supposition don't really matter. All that matters is cycling through the tests, getting the cold, hard data, and enjoying the increases in response and therefore income!

The Same Concept Applies to Ads

So, these landing pages we've been talking about? Know how people get to them? Especially if we're focusing on paid traffic? That's right — ads! And you'll definitely want to apply the magic of split testing to ads as well. Here's why…

Ad Example #1: Cleaner and More Direct Ad Skyrockets CTR (click-through rate) by 433%!

This example of Humana health insurance company again illustrates the power of testing vastly different approaches as a starting point. The control version is above; and the new version below has tighter ad copy, an image of a couple rather than an individual, and a bolder call to action button, among other things. The result of the test was that the new version had a whopping 433% higher click-through rate than the first one! That's more than four times the visitors to your landing page from the same cost per click on your ad! Are you starting to see how this testing business can be a colossal game-changer?

As with landing pages, our process for ads is:

- Test several different conceptual approaches.
- Take the winning version and start running A/B tests where only one variable is changed.
- The winner from Step 2 becomes the "control" to test new versions against, and it's an ongoing process.

The Humana example above illustrates Step 1 and produces a massive 433% increase in CTR. Now, let's look at an example of how Step 2 plays out:

Ad Example #2: Adding an Emoji Increases CTR By 241%

Version 1:

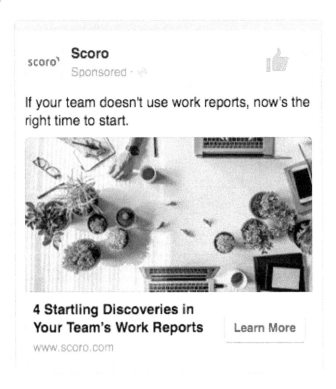

Version 2: The only change is adding a flag emoji before the "4 Startling Discoveries..." text:

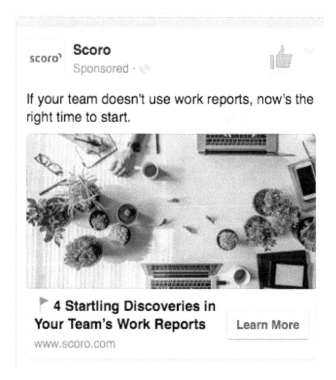

Compare versions one and two of this ad test that Scoro (London-based business management software company) ran, and you'll see that the text, image and call-to-action buttons are exactly the same on both ads. Literally the only difference is the flag emoji. It's astounding that just adding in the emoji caused a 241% increase in CTR, but the numbers don't lie and that's exactly what happened!

Now Let's Look at Sales

If testing different versions of our ads and landing pages can yield such dramatic results, it stands to reason that we can also do some serious damage with our actual sales conversion, right?! Let's find out. ☺

Sales Example #1: Focusing on Credibility Over Price Increases Sales 107%

Let's look at a simple yet show-stopping example from Express Watches — a UK-based seller of Seiko watches. Here's their original sales page, in which they make the decision to compete on price, emphasizing that they're "Never Beaten on Price."

Now let's look at the test version:

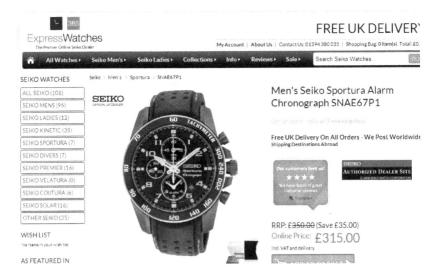

Can you spot the difference? If you said "Authorized Seiko Dealer" instead of "Never Beaten on Price," congrats! If not, no worries — such a "minor" change is easy to miss. Except in this case, it turned out to very much *not* be minor. Changing that small box to be credibility-based rather than price-based turned out to cause an amazing 107% increase in conversion! Can you imagine doubling your sales just by changing a few words around?

Sales Example #2: Highlighting a Discount Boosts Conversion by 148.3% *Without* Lowering the Price!

Check out this remarkable test conducted by The Corkscrew Wine Merchants in Ireland. As you'll see, both offers are for the exact same bottle of wine. You'll also notice that both the regular price and the discount price are the same in both versions, but in version two, the discount was highlighted while in version one it wasn't. Just the mere inclusion of the red circle saying "15% off" boosted conversions by a phenomenal 148.3%!

Version 1:

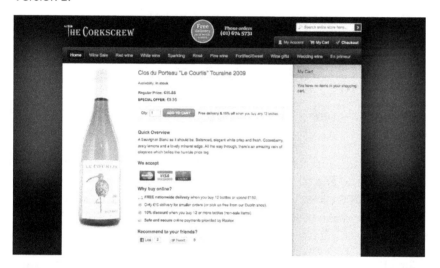

Version 2:

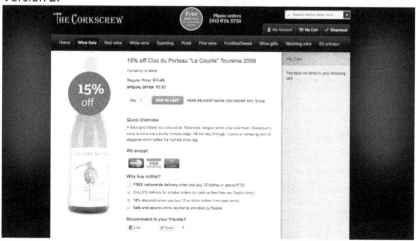

The most powerful (and liberating!) thing to remember here is that you do NOT need to know anything about marketing or business to run split tests. Just use your imagination, common sense, and all the data you gathered on your market with your 3D glasses research! And as we continue our journey together, I'll be happy to give you all kinds of things you can test as well.

There's really very little downside to running a new test. You'll always have your control version. If the new version doesn't beat it, just keep running the control until you think of another test to try out!

How to Multiply Your Bank Account With Far More Conservative Numbers Than the Examples Above

OK, let's look at a very realistic scenario of how your numbers and testing flow can go with *far* smaller boosts in your numbers than the examples I've just shared with you.

Remember, our flow here is **ads > landing pages > sales pages**. Let's take 'em in order!

So, we start with ads. Just for the purposes of easy math, let's say you spend $100 on your first ad and do no testing at all (which you'd never actually do, right?! :) and get 100 clicks, which means your baseline cost per click is $1.00 per click. Trust me when I say this is extremely conservative. More often than not, you'll be able to get clicks for under $1.00 even with **bad ads**.

From your $1.00 per click baseline, let's say that you run split tests (changing one variable only) with four elements of your ads:

- You test different audiences
- You test different images and/or videos
- You test different headlines
- You test different body text

I've found it not uncommon to see doubling and tripling of response rate in each of these four categories by properly going through the testing process. But let's be a LOT more conservative, and say that each of these tests delivers you a 25% boost rather than the 433% and 241% increases in the case studies above.

Now, let's put some dollars and cents to this...

With the first ad you run, before you go through this testing process, you're paying $1 per click.

If you get a 25% increase in response from each of the four elements I mentioned above (audience, image/video, headline and body text), here's the breakdown of how your cost per click drops:

Baseline: 100 clicks = **$1.00 per click**

Audience Test: 25% boost = 125 clicks = **$0.80 per click** ($1.00/125)

Image/video Test: 25% boost = 156 clicks = **$0.64 per click**

Headline Test: 25% boost = 195 clicks = **$0.51 per click**

Text (ad copy) Test: 25% boost = 244 clicks = **$0.41 per click**

This means that you're now able to pay 41 cents per visitor instead of one dollar — less than half the cost you started with! Put another way, for every $100 you spend on traffic, you'd now get 244 visitors to your site instead of 100!

Now, let's move on to the second step of our flow: **ads > landing pages > sales pages**

Let's review for a minute...

These 244 clicks you're now able to get for every $100 you spend on traffic? Where do they go? To a landing page! And what's the purpose of a landing page? To connect with your audience, grab their attention, and get them to take your MDA (Most Desired Action). Your MDA could be a number of different things, depending on your business model. But the most common MDA of a landing page is getting people to opt in to your email list, so let's roll with that for this illustration.

So, let's say that in the initial version of your landing page, you get an opt-in rate of 20%. In other words, 20 out of every 100 people who visit your landing page join your email list. Before you ran your ad tests, you were paying $1.00 per click initially in this example, so for every $100 you spend, you get 100 visitors and 20 opt-ins to your email list. So, out of the gate you're paying $5 per opt-in.

Not a bad start, but...

With the work you did on your ads to get your per-click cost down from $1.00 to 41 cents, you're now getting 244 visitors to your landing page. Meaning that with the same 20% opt-in rate, you'd now get 49 opt-ins. So, you're now paying around two dollars ($2.04 to be exact: $100/49) per opt-in rather than $5.00! Huuuuuge improvement. ☺

Again, these are all extremely realistic — even conservative — numbers, provided of course that you do the work to go through the testing process.

Now, let's continue and be *even more conservative...*

Let's say you go through a similar testing process with your landing page — whether testing entirely different versions as I did with my Ultimate Vida landing pages I showed you in the last chapter, or with far simpler tests like different headlines, colors, opt-in buttons, etc. Let's say this process yields you nowhere near the 102.5% or 38.26% increases in the two examples above, but a far more conservative 20% increase. And rather than the four bumps in response you got from your ad testing, let's say you're only able to get two bumps of 20% this time around with your landing pages. Of course, you wouldn't actually stop testing, so your bumps should continue — but we want to be conservative here.

Here's how the numbers would play out:

Baseline before ad testing: $100 = 100 visitors @20% opt-in rate = 20 opt-ins = **$5.00 per opt-in**

Baseline after ad testing: $100 = 244 visitors @20% opt-in rate = 49 opt-ins = **$2.04 per opt-in**

Landing page test #1: 244 visitors @ 24% opt-in rate (20% increase) = 59 opt-ins = **$1.69 per opt-in**

Landing page test #2: 244 visitors @ 29% opt-in rate (20% increase) = 71 opt-ins = **$1.41 per opt-in**

Just to quickly review the power of what's going on here: You've cycled through your ad tests and landing page tests, and you're now paying *less than a third* of your original cost per opt-in ($5 down to $1.41). Put another way, every marketing dollar you spend now stretches **more than three times as far**!

But we're not done yet. Not by a long shot. Because we haven't even talked about the most important part of this equation — sales! After all, the whole point of running ads and getting visitors to your landing page is to have them take an action (joining your email list, filling out a form, calling you, etc.) which eventually ends up with you selling a product or service and making money.

Ads > landing pages > sales pages

With an eye towards sales, let's take your initial baseline before your testing where for every $100 you spend, you get 100 visitors to your landing page and 20 people on your email list.

Now, let's say that the first offer you make to these people costs $50 and has a 2% conversion rate — meaning 2% of the people who see the offer buy. And let's further say (again, in the spirit of being conservative) that you only make this offer to people who've joined your list.

Your initial numbers would look like this:

- $100 spent
- 100 visitors
- 20 opt-ins
- 2% of the 20 make a purchase for $50, which equals .4 sales (obviously you can't have a fraction of a sale, but we're just using simple numbers here to illustrate a point)
- .4x$50 = $20

So, you've spent $100 and only made $20 back. Ouch, ouch, ouch! Right? This is where I'd usually hear things like:

"I've only made back 20% of what I spent — terrible!"

"I've lost 80% — this is clearly not working!"

Or worst of all...

"I'm not even anywhere close to succeeding. I better scrap this offer or maybe scrap this business altogether, or maybe even *scrap the idea of going into business for myself.*"

I can't tell you how often I see and hear scenarios just like this one. And every time I do, it breaks my heart.

My language-learning client told me that before we started working together, he once spent $100 on an ad for his Spanish course, and made $100 back; and he felt so stressed out and unsuccessful, he basically put his (actually brilliant) Spanish course on the back-burner for over THREE YEARS.

Three years of delay. *Ouch*.

Now, if I'm lucky enough to have communication with the person going through this tough stage, I'll pivot faster than you can blink to "Don't give up! You're actually **far closer than you think** — all you have to do is test, test, test!"

Here's why...

Through the testing example I've already taken you through, remember we've gotten up to 71 opt-ins from the same $100 spent on traffic.

So, with the same 2% sales conversion rate on our $50 product, instead of making $10 back on our $100, we now make 1.42 sales (71 people x 2%).

1.42 x $50 = $71. Now we're getting somewhere! We're not profitable yet, but we're getting dangerously close. We're now at $71 back for every $100 spent — or 71 cents for every dollar spent.

Now, what happens if we do some testing on our actual sales message? What happens if we go through a similar process as we did with our landing page and, rather than achieving a 148.3% or 107% boost like the examples above, we again get two bumps of 20% each? I'm not saying these increases will happen overnight — but I *am* saying that these are again quite conservative figures if you actually go through the testing process and are consistent and persistent.

Let's see what happens...

Baseline before ad tests: $100 = 100 visitors = 20 opt-ins = .4 sales @$50 = $20 in sales = **$80 loss**

Baseline after ad tests: $100 = 244 visitors = 49 opt-ins = 1 sale @$50 = $50 in sales = **$50 loss**

Baseline after landing page tests: $100 = 244 visitors = 71 opt-ins = 1.42 sales @$50 = $71 in sales = **$29 loss**

Sales test #1: $100 = 244 visitors = 71 opt-ins = 1.7 sales @$50 (2.4%

conversion instead of 2%) = $85 in sales = **$15 loss**

Sales test #2: $100 = 244 visitors = 71 opt-ins = 2 sales @ $50 (2.9% conversion) = $100 in sales = **breakeven**

Two sales at $50 is some easy math indeed — $100! And what was our spend? $100! BOOM! We are now in breakeven territory!

You may be thinking "Ummmm ok, what's so exciting about spending $100 to make $100?"

(Hint: Remember the BMG Music and Wall Street Wines examples in the "Knowing Everybody's Routines" chapter? A **$1.4 Billion** company was built by *losing money* on the front end, and you're now breaking even, which is far better!)

Put another way, breaking even on your ad spend means **free customer acquisition**!

What Happens After You Make the First Sale?

Let's continue down this path by making the key point that you are NOT going to stop the customer's journey with you after making the first sale — **ever**. Making the first sale to a customer is by far the hardest sale to make. Once someone has become a customer and you've given them value and earned their trust, selling additional solutions to them becomes far easier.

So, let's say that you sell a slightly higher-priced product to your existing customers which solves a different problem they have and this time costs them $100 rather than $50. And let's say that you only get a 1% conversion rate this time around rather than your 2% conversion rate (which you increased to 2.9% through testing) the first time around. Let's further say that you get lazy here and don't do any additional testing to boost that conversion rate, so it stays at 1% (which you'd never actually do, right?). ☺

This means that one out of every hundred customers would spend an additional $100 — or put another way, your average value per customer just increased by $1.

Guess what this does to our initial investment in traffic? Now, instead of spending $100 and getting $100 back, you've spent $100 and gotten $200 back! DOUBLE BOOM! Literally. You've now **doubled your money**. And more importantly, you've done so in a predictable, scalable and data-driven manner. You've now created a machine where for every dollar you put in, you get two dollars back.

I just have one question for you: How many dollars would you feed into that machine? And more important than the money itself — do you see how creating these machines will **set you free**?

Let me stress again that the example I just took you through are hypothetical numbers. But I can say hand on heart that this kind of scenario is very doable. Sure, you may not get a 2% sales conversion right out of the gate. But on the flip side, it's also quite common for your baseline cost per click to be far lower than $1.00. And if you are relentless with testing, it's entirely possible for you to do far better than the 20% bumps I referenced. The examples above — and many others like them — prove it.

It's also likely that you wouldn't stop at just one back-end offer. If you did, it would be kind of crazy. In fact, if you take care of your email list in the manner we've drilled down on in this book, it is reasonable to expect around 50 cents per month per subscriber in income. So, as you see, there are many paths to creating these virtual ATM machines.

Bonus: Two Advanced Traffic Strategies *Not* for the Faint of Heart

Advanced Traffic Strategy #1: Make Money by Selling... *Nothing?*

Remember how I mentioned earlier in the book that you can actually make money online without selling anything at all?

It's absolutely true. There are a number of models for doing this. But the one that's by far the most achievable for regular non-techy folks like you and me is making money via **ad revenue.**

Put simply, if you have a website on a topic of interest to a certain group of people... and you're able to drive traffic to that site (whether paid traffic or free)... and it's a topic (market) where products and services are bought and sold? Then you can literally make money by simply allowing companies like Google (yes, Google!) to place relevant ads on your site. And then Google will pay you a certain amount of money every time anyone on your site clicks one of the ads!

Why would Google want to do this? To illustrate this model, let's talk about a site I used to own...

So, you may or may not remember that back in the day, Microsoft Word documents used to have the extension .doc. And then with a newer version of Word, the extension changed to .docx. Does this ring a bell? Anyway, it happened. ☺

What also happened here is that there were suddenly swarms of people who urgently needed to get their .doc files converted to .docx files. And I had a site that did this for people for free. They could simply upload their .doc file on my site and voila, my site would automatically convert it to .docx and they'd be a happy camper!

But you know what else happened on that site? Trusty ol' Google placed a few relevant ads for document conversion and other technology services. Where did they get these ads from? From companies in industries related to the topic of my site who wanted to advertise there and were willing to pay every time someone clicked! As you might imagine, a fair amount of people clicked on the ads. After all, why wouldn't they? The ads were relevant and related to what they were interested in. And every time someone clicked one of the ads on my site? Google would pay me a piece of that click and keep a piece for itself.

How much was each click worth? That always has been and always will be dynamic. It depends on the marketplace and changes by the second. It's based on supply and demand and what the advertisers of these services are willing to pay every time someone clicks on one of their ads. Depending on the market and its conditions, clicks can be worth anywhere from a few cents to $10 or more.

This model is still alive and well today (Google happily promotes it at https://www.google.com/adsense/start/), and I dare say it always will be. Think of it like this. Since the beginning of print, newspapers and magazines have accepted and even solicited ads in their publications. Well, a website — whether a general news/media site, or a site targeted to a certain group or topic — is simply an electronic publication! And there's no reason the site can't collect ad revenue as well. Companies who sell products and services to the avatar (there's that concept again!) who visits that site would obviously be interested in advertising there. So it's a win/win. ☺

The other cool thing about this model? It totally lends itself to building an online tribe and crafting your Ultimate Vida, which is the central focus of this book. The core concept of selecting hungry markets and passionate groups of people and deeply connecting with them absolutely applies whether you're directly selling anything to them or not. As evidenced by this Google AdSense model, it doesn't necessarily have to be **you** doing the selling — you just have to make sure that money's changing hands within the market.

So why do I say this strategy is not for the faint of heart? I mean, it kind of sounds less risky, right? You don't have to sell any products or services, and you don't even have to buy traffic!

But remember what I said about organic traffic usually being far harder to generate than paid, and even more difficult to sustain or scale? Well, that's still the case no matter what the objective of your website is. So, by all means if you're talented in driving traffic organically or happen to have a big email list or social media following? Then this model can absolutely work. But my general recommendation to stick with paid traffic and selling your own products & services (where you keep 100% of the revenues, I might add, rather than sharing them with Google or anyone else) still stands.

So, how — you might ask — did I wind up with this document conversion site, if I prefer paid traffic to free **and** I am famously non-technical?

Well…

Advanced Traffic Strategy #2: Digital Real Estate

So, here's the thing. I didn't build the document conversion site. How could I with my lack of tech skills? Nor did I have someone create it for me. *I bought it.* For $10,000. That sounds like a lot of money, and it is. But for several years in a row, I made a minimum of $1,000 per month **from this site alone**, and at the peak I was making around $3k per month. The time required for me to run the site? Zero. It literally ran itself. How is that possible? Because it had very strong and consistent search engine traffic, as well as a bunch of links all over the Internet. In other words, organic traffic. And it made money from traffic rather than selling anything, so there were no customers or support.

It's hard to even wrap my head around the return I was making on my investment on this site and others like it. Even at the low end of $1,000 per month, I was making a 120% annual return on my investment. That's just insane. Most investors are very happy with anything over 10%. And it's not like I swindled the previous owner out of the site. He was thrilled to sell it to me for $10,000. You'd be surprised how many people start a website as a "hobby business" and are startled when they start making a bit of cash from it. But then they realize that they have no interest in managing and sustaining it. And on top of that, "real life" hits them and they realize they could use some cash so they put their site up for sale because it's their only asset. At the time he sold it, $10,000 was some serious "found money" for the previous owner. I had done my due diligence and verified how much traffic he was getting, and I knew I could monetize it better than he could. It was a total win-win.

The other main benefit is that it completely eliminates the need for the 3D glasses research. This is staggeringly powerful. As powerful (and fun!) as the research and validation process is that I've shown you in this book? Imagine if you could skip it altogether and not only know that your site would make money, but start making that money right from Day 1. That's what becomes possible when you buy websites with existing cash flow.

For a good few years, buying and selling websites was my main focus. I called it digital real estate because I would look for websites (i.e. online properties) that already had an existing cash flow and required little or no maintenance.

And then I'd either flip them for an immediate profit, hold onto them and enjoy the monthly cash flow; or, if I was feeling ambitious, occasionally I'd do some work to improve the site and increase the earnings.

This business model treated me very well, and I made a great deal of money from it. But eventually I reached a point where it just wasn't fulfilling. Yes, I enjoyed the cash flow and financial rewards, but I just wasn't feeling excited or motivated about my work or that I was making an impact on people. And that just didn't feel good so I stopped doing it.

But the model itself? It still works extremely well today, and yes, it'll still work swimmingly years from now. Again, it's timeless! People have been buying and selling property for centuries, and websites are simply digital properties with far fewer hassles and headaches than actual property.

Why then, am I recommending buying and selling websites as a sideline option that's "not for the faint of heart" rather than as one of my core strategies? Well, because it's risky! First of all, you can and will lose money at times if you do this. When I did this, I picked winners more often than not, but I certainly took some painful losses. No one — and I mean *no one* — has a 100% success rate. And when you get one wrong, it'll sting financially.

Secondly, when you buy existing business, they tend to have a lot more moving parts. They're rarely anywhere near as simple as the digital tribal model that we've outlined in great detail in this book. My document conversion site was the exception, not the rule!

Thirdly, it can be challenging to do your due diligence and make sure the revenue and traffic figures that the seller claims are accurate. And if you've never done this before, even more so.

Finally, and most importantly, when you hit that "existential crisis" I've mentioned — or even when you reach the point where money alone does not fulfill you — it'll be much harder to sustain your excitement and momentum.

For all these reasons, I'm not going to go into great detail on the nitty-gritty tactics of how to buy and sell sites successfully and stack the odds in your favor at this time. Maybe if enough of you express interest, I'll do a special course or workshop on it or something. But for now, it is NOT my main recommendation for you. But it was a key part of what I did, so I felt I owed it to you to at least give you an overview. And I absolutely see it as a wise move for you in the future once you've created and sustained your Ultimate Vida for a while and want to move into building an investment portfolio. And when that time comes? I'll have your back and help you make it happen.

Once You Hit Upon a Winning Formula, It's Scale Baby, Scale

It's easy to get seduced by organic traffic. After all, it's "free!" But is it really? Not by a long shot.

First of all, getting serious organic traffic is hard. You either have to be an expert at SEO (search engine optimization), social media, blogging or public relations.

And even if you are an expert in one of these areas? The traffic is still not truly free. Why? Because it takes time. And time is money.

But most painful of all? Even if you *are* an expert and are willing to put in the time... it is really not scalable. Meaning you can hit upon a winning formula... be getting quality organic traffic... maybe even be making some money... but what happens when you want to double or triple your traffic and income? Not to mention 5x or 10x it?

With organic traffic, it's damn near impossible.

But with paid traffic?

It's kind of like cranking up the faucet or putting more fuel on the fire. The higher you turn it up, the more juice you get out of it.

I have a friend and client in the UK, and we have literally increased his spending on paid traffic by 25x in the past three months, and — not surprisingly! — both his revenues and profits are at an all-time high. Now, he's gone out and employed a couple of new staff members straight away, before he had a big enough surplus in the bank (he calls himself an idiot for that, but I think it was a wise move!), so we've still got some work to do there — but paid traffic is going to save his bacon and get him to seven figures this year.

Is there any other reliable way to scale a business by even two or three times in just a few months, let alone 25x? I think not.

Learn paid traffic, control your income and control your life. Simple as that.

Most Importantly, Paid Traffic = FREEDOM

The money part of paid traffic is nice. Very nice. It's pretty damn cool to be able to "control your income," in a sense.

But what's even cooler?

Controlling your lifestyle. Controlling your time. Controlling your *freedom.*

With organic, even if you're highly skilled – which very few people are; I know I'm not – you've got to constantly be in hustle mode for the next big "hit." The next surge of traffic.

But if you're willing to buy your traffic? Create that "Internet ATM machine" where you put in $1 and get out $1.50? Or maybe even $2 or $3?

That's where the real fun starts.

That's where you get to crank up the faucet and reap the rewards.

That's where you get to truly taste freedom.

Because I assure you, it takes FAR less time per day to manage and optimize your ads (or pay an expert to do it) with guaranteed targeted traffic than it does to be hustling for organic traffic that may or may not come.

And this, my friend, is how you start to truly create your freedom lifestyle. How you get to finally call your own shots, and live on your own terms. Work the hours you choose from the location you choose. Live your Ultimate Vida.

Oh, and a fun little bonus of paid traffic? Charge said traffic to a rewards-earning credit card, and before you know it, you'll be earning enough points and miles for first class travel and five-star accommodations. This can be worth tens of thousands of dollars per year in its own right, and allow you to see the world, which is priceless!

Where to Buy Your Traffic

With all this talk about testing different ads, landing pages, and sales pages – not to mention my shouting from the rooftops "buy your traffic!" – you might be thinking, "OK Jesse, I hear you, but where the heck should I buy my traffic from?"

As usual, I'm glad you asked :). And I've got two answers for you...

The first answer is that this is where your SimilarWeb research comes into play. Remember those other sites in your space that you ran through

SimilarWeb? And it gave you the exact breakdown of where they're getting their traffic from? I'd say it would be very hard to go wrong buying traffic from the same sources that the major players in your space are buying from.

My second answer is that if the SimilarWeb research doesn't give you a crystal clear picture, or if you have any doubts whatsoever about where to get your traffic from, I'd suggest starting with Facebook Ads. I've been buying traffic for 22 years, and Facebook is by far the most robust ad platform I've ever worked with, and has the best targeting capabilities to boot.

I could easily write an entire book on Facebook ads (I've spent tens of millions of dollars on their platform — yikes!), but to get started, just head over to https://www.facebook.com/business/ads. Unlike many online platforms, Facebook actually has incredibly clear and helpful tutorials that'll have you up and running in no time, even if you're a techno-moron like me :)

My guidance won't stop there, however. I've certainly got some tricks up my sleeve that you won't find in the tutorials. Stuff I've learned along the way from my mistakes, my successes, and driving hundreds of millions of clicks. I'll point you in the right direction on the UV resource page I've been referring to throughout this book, which you can find at www.ultimateviada.com/toolbox.

Action Steps
Check them off - literally, in ink!

Use your 3D research file to choose an audience for your first ad

Choose and image or a video and some simple clear text for your first ad

Spend $20 on your first ad and find out your starting cost per click

Your Moment of Truth

I suppose this is when I'm supposed to tell you something like "If you keep doing what you've been doing, you'll keep getting what you've always gotten."

Or maybe on a more practical note, I should advise you to set your alarm an hour earlier or cut out your favorite TV show.

It's not that this is bad advice. In a vacuum, it makes sense and can work.

But I'm not going to go there with you.

Maybe you value your sleep more than just about anything (I sure do!).

Or, maybe your favorite show uplifts and inspires you.

But if there's one judgment of your character that I *do* feel qualified to make, it's that you have extraordinary courage.

The amount of resolve, independent thinking and inner work it took to even get to the point where you were curious enough to pick up this book took serious guts. And that's before you even opened a single page.

But to make it all the way to the end? To come this far down the rabbit hole with me? To be seriously considering making such a seismic shift that can completely change the equation of what's possible in your life?

That is big time stuff. I have such mad respect for you. I wish I could look you in the eye right now, raise a glass to you, and celebrate all that you are and all that's about to unfold for you. Hopefully one day I'll get that chance.

But in the here and now, rather than me giving you clichéd advice, however well-intentioned, let's take a different approach.

Your One-Year Crystal Ball

Let's pretend you have a crystal ball that reveals what your life will be like one year from now; in exactly 365 days.

Obviously, we can't know all the details. But we can paint the broad strokes. What would be the lead story? The headline, if you will?

Would it be presumptuous of me to guess that it just might be that you've left your job and your time is now your own?

To think that you've made it to the end of this book for the quality of my writing or any other reason — now *that* would feel presumptuous!

And for me to tell you how quickly or slowly to do it, or what adjustments you may need to make to your life (or not) to make it happen? That would feel even more presumptuous. That's entirely your decision. You've earned that right.

So, the only thing we're left with, is how are you going to do it?

I believe that the path has been clearly illuminated in this book.

I would have given anything to have a book and roadmap like this when I set out to create my Ultimate Vida. It's no stretch to say that I would have saved several years of time and hundreds of thousands of dollars had I known and followed the blueprint in this book.

Some Good News and Some Real Talk

First, the good news. This book is a complete blueprint to build an online tribe that earns you the income to leave your job whenever you choose.

I can say with a very clear conscience that I have followed my own rule and that this book passes the "Mom test." Meaning that if my mom or anyone I love asked me how to generate an income online and live the life of their choosing, I would give them this book.

You may well be able to take this book, follow the steps, and create a life so glorious that you'll have to constantly pinch yourself to see if it's real.

If you do, nothing would make me happier. All I'd ask in this case is that you drop me a note sometime at jesse@ultimatevida.com and tell me your story. You and your success stories are the fuel to my fire; the wind beneath my wings.

Now for the Real Talk

Did I include every last detail of how to implement each step in this book?

Of course not. That would have been impossible. This book would have gotten uncomfortably long and detailed, made it less likely that you read it all the way through, and ultimately done you a disservice.

Not to mention, it would have been as thick as the Bible or "War and Peace!"

The responsibility of a book is to provide a blueprint and roadmap. I believe this book has accomplished that, and then some. You could very well follow the blueprint and achieve even better results than I have. If you do, I'll be your biggest cheerleader!

What I also know to be true is that there have been a few times when I have read books that deeply impacted me, and wished the author had an even more detailed guide available with all the nitty-gritty details, "how to" steps, and success markers that would increase my odds of success. So, I've decided to provide that to you in the form of the Ultimate Vida course, which you can check out at www.UltimateVida.com/toolbox.

Let's Get Even More Real

I'm not going to pretend money doesn't matter. Of course it does. Nor am I going to pretend that I can make a profit just by putting this book in your hands.

Spoiler alert. I can't. In fact, it's just the opposite. I'm actually *losing* money to get this book in your hands. It was a conscious decision I made, eyes wide open.

There are two reasons for this:

First, I'm aware that you and I didn't know each other before this book (hopefully you feel a bit differently now!), and therefore it did not feel right to charge more than a nominal amount to get this book in your hands. The responsibility of earning your trust was squarely on my shoulders — right where it belongs.

Secondly, I made a promise to myself to offer insane value — a minimum of 10x the price and ideally 1000x or more — in any product I bring to the marketplace.

I believe this book has delivered on that promise and could be worth an unlimited amount to you if you take what's in these pages and implement it. In fact, I believe you'd be hard-pressed to find any book in the world that offers you more actionable tips on how to leave your job and create your own freedom-based lifestyle.

I also know that there's a chance you'll want even higher-level and more detailed advice, hand-holding, success markers, accountability and more.

And I know that if enough of you take that chance with me — as I have with my mentors — it will increase your odds of success and once again be worth many times what you pay. And that it will also allow me to gratefully do what I love, which is teach and facilitate this blueprint to freedom seekers around the world. Put another way, it'll allow me to make a living from building a tribe, just as the blueprint in this book lays out! If that's not a beautiful cycle based in love and integrity, I don't know what is :)

The Elephant in the Room

I have a good idea what you might be thinking at this moment, so let's bring it out into the open and see if I'm right...

When I just said the bit about "It'll allow me to earn a living from building a tribe, just as the blueprint in this book lays out?"

You might've been thinking "Hmmmm, yeah that's fair — a guy's gotta earn a living... but hang on, wait a minute... if Jesse's been doing this for 22 years and had all these different businesses, isn't he already making a good living? And if he's not, whoa — should I even be listening to him?"

Look, I'd be having that exact same inner dialogue if I were reading this book. It's completely fair and natural.

So, let me take you behind the curtain and be radically transparent with you...

I have indeed been fortunate to earn a very good living for 22 years now by following the formula I've shown you in this book.

I've had online businesses in markets ranging from baby names, classic cars, document conversion, web design templates, golf, and many, many more.

Heck, I even built an online business and tribe about knitting (yes, knitting!), and later sold that business for a nice 6-figure sum.

You might not be surprised to discover that I don't know the first thing about knitting. I've never knit anything in my life, nor read a single book about knitting. But as I revealed earlier in this book, I went through a phase when I didn't build businesses around my passions.

During that phase, knitting checked all the boxes in our research process (which was nowhere near as refined as the one you're holding in your hands right now!) and we were able to build a nice business and tribe around it, not to mention bring joy to knitting enthusiasts around the world.

We created a fictitious female character (based on the avatar formula I've shared with you) to be the face of this knitting business. And it worked very well. But like other non-passion businesses, I just wasn't feeling excited about it, so eventually I stopped. Which is why I'm so bullish about building a tribe around a topic that actually lights you up.

I've also earned quite a bit of income over the years consulting for various businesses, coaching business owners on their marketing, and running paid traffic campaigns. (Side note and potential "aha" moment for you: I've done this, by the way, using the concepts I've shared with you in this book about strategy, tactics, storytelling, landing pages and paid traffic!)

This has allowed me to basically get clients on demand and get paid very well for helping people grow their businesses.

But a few years ago, when I least expected it, something very interesting happened...

I decided to join an online tribe for business owners around the world — yes, there's that tribal concept again!

Over the years, I've had various mentors and people who've helped me out in one form or another. And I really wanted to give back and "pay it forward."

I saw a post from a gentleman in Wales who owns a language learning company and was having some challenges with his Facebook ad campaigns. It just so happened that I've spent many millions of dollars on Facebook ads and know the platform inside out. So, I offered to hop on a call with him and help him out.

That call ended up lasting almost two hours, and as I later found out, he was shocked that I didn't try to sell him anything. Honestly, it never even occurred to me to do so.

(Remember, we want to start from a place of B.O.S.S. (Be of Supreme Service) and blow people away with the value we provide.)

If you're able to do that, and genuinely show you care? Trust me when I say the financial floodgates will open without your having to try so hard.

Anyway, he and I had a few more calls and it turned out that we had a tremendous amount of synergy. I mentioned to him that I'm in the UK on business a fair amount, and I'd be happy to take a train up to Wales the next time I was "across the pond" so that we could meet in person and deepen our discussions.

I did that a few months later and hit it off not only with him, but also his wife and kids. One thing led to another and we began working together on a regular basis. I started by running his Facebook ads, but it soon became evident to both of us that I had a lot more to offer and was doing him and his business a disservice by only running his ads. So, I started acting as a strategic advisor to him not only on marketing, but other elements of growing and running a business as well — applying what I'd learned over the years in running my own businesses.

We've had quite a run over the past few years and have experienced phenomenal growth. He recently surprised me by offering me a small equity position in his company. I gratefully accepted.

But you want to know the kicker?

He and I are very much aligned when it comes to exchanging value for money rather than time for money. So, he doesn't particularly care how many hours I spend as long as I help to grow and steer his company which is what I was brought on to do.

And he is not only aware of, but enthusiastically supports my writing this book and building the Ultimate Vida tribe.

(More on that in a moment, with a surprise twist that you won't see coming!)

At the time of this book's publication, I earn a decent income from working with his company, but not enough to support the lifestyle I'm accustomed to (which basically means frequent world travel — I don't much care about luxury or material items).

I have every expectation that this income stream will eventually grow into a significant amount.

But until it does? I've got a few options...

I could seek out a few more clients to help with their marketing and/or run their ad campaigns. This would be fairly easy, as it's right in my wheelhouse and I always deliver tremendous value.

Alternatively, I could run some affiliate marketing campaigns and/or start a new side business, following the exact formula I've shared with you in this book!

I am extremely confident that either of these options would be successful.

But I see two major problems with choosing one of these options...

First of all, they don't light me up. I wouldn't have that "Can't wait to get up and do this; gives me chills" feeling.

Secondly, and more importantly?

Neither of these options serve YOU in any way. And I simply can't live with that.

So, the third option, which is the one I'm actually going to pursue?

Build out Ultimate Vida, for God's sake!

Get this book in the hands of as many epic freedom seekers like YOU as possible.

Follow the book up with an A-to-Z course that not only shows you all the nitty-gritty details of how to actually make it happen, but also features case studies for you to model of people who've actually gone through the Ultimate Vida Blueprint and come out the other side with a successful online business that's allowed them to seize control of their lives!

Then create the most epic, badass, legendary tribe of freedom seekers on the face of this planet — a community where we can all connect. Because no matter how good the book and course are, we know that we're SO much stronger together when we're part of a tribe with common goals and dreams.

You'll get to freedom faster, enjoy the ride more and have greater clarity if you do it as part of a tribe. It's that simple.

And do you remember that "existential crisis" I mentioned in the intro of this book?

Well...as hard as it may be to believe it right now, you WILL hit it. Mark my words. And that's when the tribe will shine even brighter for you. That's when the tribe will lift you up and carry you through.

Don't worry, you probably won't hit this crisis for a while.

First, you'll be laser focused on crafting your "escape plan" and getting to freedom.

Then, you'll enjoy a "freedom honeymoon" that'll last anywhere from a few months to a few years where you're just so damn happy to be in control of your own life again that nothing else really matters.

But somewhere along the way, you WILL come face to face with your inner self.

Maybe it'll be intense like mine was, or maybe it'll be more of a dull emptiness or confusion.

But you WILL reach a point where you're feeling "OK, I'm free. That's awesome. But what's next?"

And when you do?

That's when you'll be able to tap into entirely new dimensions of your Ultimate Vida tribe.

That's when we'll explore not only achieving freedom through building online businesses...

But also dive into optimizing your life and getting you feeling whole and complete.

We'll dive into health, relationships, finances, spirituality, and yes, language learning — and much more — together.

We'll dive into uncovering what YOUR Ikigai looks like and how to take your freedom lifestyle to the next level that revolves around it and gives you the ultimate joy and meaning.

Make no mistake, my friend. We're just getting started. I am fully determined for Ultimate Vida to be your core, your anchor, your guiding light; the ride of your life with you firmly at the steering wheel, charting your own course that is uniquely YOU.

Beyond the book, course and community, who knows where Ultimate Vida will go!

I wouldn't be surprised at all if we start doing live events, meetups around the world, coaching, and even open up the Ultimate Vida Ambassador Program where YOU could become a UV coach to help others achieve freedom too!

But if there's one thing I DO know?

It's that the direction we take will be determined by YOU.

And if there's another thing I know?

It's that I'm in this forever.

This is my life's work and mission and I'll never leave you hanging.

So, how does this come full circle with the "elephant in the room" that I called myself out on at the beginning of this chapter?

Well, it basically means that I've got multiple ways I can support myself financially, but going "all in" with Ultimate Vida is not only my preferred way, but more importantly the path that I believe allows me to be of the highest service to YOU.

And how does this come full circle with my dear friend and client in Wales who owns the language learning company?

It's almost too crazy to even be true...

Not only does he embrace Ultimate Vida...

Not only do we both see all kinds of synergy between Ultimate Vida and language learning, both in business and life...

Not only is setting people free one of our shared creeds and passions in life...

But guess who I am honored and privileged to have as my editor of this book you are now reading?

That's right — Aran Jones, co-founder of SaySomethingin.com!

Oh, and as I'm writing these very words to you to complete this book and get it in your hands? I'm on a plane with him to China where we're going to have high-level meetings about teaching English to over a billion people in China. Talk about setting people free!

If that doesn't bring full circle the tribal concept, being of service, treating people like family, and everything else we've talked about in this book, I don't know what possibly could :)

My ultimate dream and desire is for Ultimate Vida to transform your life and to be the final tribe I build.

If you allow me this privilege, it will be the honor of my lifetime.

Let's do this!

-Jesse

Your Checklist — To Keep Yourself on Track

I know I've crammed this book full of detail — steps you can and should take to win your personal freedom.

But I also know it can be easy to get overwhelmed — to think "Yeah, that was all good, but I can't even remember where to get started now!"

So this final checklist is a summary of what we've covered — so you can see at a glance where you are and what you need to do next.

1. Make a list of what you're good at, and what you love doing

2. Choose one topic from that list, and research it — in Udemy, Amazon, Facebook and online forums

3. Build an avatar

4. List and research your competitors, and buy the entry-level product for three key players in your field

5. Choose your daily "domino" action

6. Start recording a daily piece of micro-content for your audience

7. Solve a burning problem for 10 different people, and document the process

8. Package the process as a document that people can buy for a low cost, featuring the success stories of people who you've solved the burning problem for.

9. Choose your tech tools to create a place for your tribe

10. Test your first ad

11. Share your results in the Ultimate Vida community for feedback and support

And as always, any info, links or resources where you feel like you're missing some level of detail that was too much for the book to go into, I've got you covered over at www.UltimateVida.com/toolbox.

Acknowledgments

Dear Reader,

It may be unconventional to start my acknowledgments by thanking "strangers," but that's not how I see you. Your courage and conviction to change your life moves me to the core. You are why I wrote this book, so how could I not start with you? I see you and feel you deeply, and I'm honored to have your back on your freedom journey.

To achieve my own freedom, naturally it took (and still takes) a tribe. There are no words that can adequately express my gratitude to the following people, but here's my shot at scratching the surface.

Mom, you've always been the heartbeat of our family and the wind beneath my wings. Now, it's my turn. I've got you.

Krys, you see me and love me for exactly who I am. That means everything, and it inspires me to be even better for you. I can't believe how fortunate I am to have the honor of loving you, mi amor.

Eli, you are so ridiculously good at so many things, little bro. You've earned everything you've gotten and done it for all the right reasons.

Rachel, you've graced our family with your heart and brilliance, and have made the ridiculously good even better.

Aran, your official title is Editor. The more accurate one feels like "brother." You've elevated this book – and my life, incalculably.

Kit, my Soul Sister – we've been around the world together, and have traveled even further within. I am so grateful for our journey, and I know the best is yet to come. In faith and friendship always.

Ramin, our concerts and trips have been epic, but our friendship even more so. Can't wait to write the next chapters, my man.

Laurie, Diana and Catrin – you are the sisters I never had. Your love and wisdom mean the world to me.

Melissa, for taking this book across the finish line and sprinkling it with your love and magic dust.

Austin and Jason, your artistry and design contributions made this book pop – thank you.

Marc, I will be forever grateful to you for bringing the initial version of Ultimate Vida to life. Your skill set is one I can only dream of. Ian and Billy, your high-level, objective input has been paramount. The three of you are Ultimate Vida men through and through, and your friendships mean even more to me than your considerable brilliance.

And to the following epic human beings, it is criminal that I don't get to write volumes about each of you, but please know how deeply I value and appreciate you:

Ajay, Andy, Arne, Carly, Cecilia, Chizzy, Cliff, Daniel, Danielle, Earnest, Edi, James, Jason, Ken, Kendra, Linh, Lorie, Marta, Matt, Michelle, Mike G., Mike M., Mitchell, Nancy, Natalie, Oliver, Patricia, Patty, Radomir, Rajeev, Ron, Scott, Stine, Yvonne.

To your freedom,

Jesse

www.ingramcontent.com/pod-product-compliance
Lightning Source LLC
Chambersburg PA
CBHW071111050326
40690CB00008B/1185